100 VEGETABLE DISHES

100 VEGETABLE DISHES

Sue Locke

OCTOPUS BOOKS

CONTENTS

Introduction 5
Hot and Cold Soups 6
Simple Starters 18
Main Courses 30
Vegetable Salads 42
Side Dishes 50
Breads and Fritters 58
Index 63

NOTES
Standard spoon measurements are used in all recipes:
1 tablespoon = one 15 ml spoon
1 teaspoon = one 5 ml spoon
All spoon measurements are level.

Where amounts of salt and pepper are unspecified in recipes the cook should use her discretion. Canned foods are used with their juices unless otherwise specified. Ovens and grills (broilers) should be preheated to the specified temperature or heat setting.
For all recipes, quantities are given in metric, imperial and American measures. Follow one set of measures only, because they are not interchangeable.

First published 1985 by
Octopus Books Limited
59 Grosvenor Street, London W1

© 1985 Octopus Books Limited

ISBN 0 7064 2315 1

Produced by Mandarin Publishers Ltd
22a Westlands Rd
Quarry Bay
Hong Kong

Printed in Hong Kong

Cover photograph:
Spring Vegetable Vol-au-Vent (see page 33)

INTRODUCTION

Vegetables are currently enjoying greater popularity than ever before.

There is an increasing awareness that a balanced, natural diet is vital for good health. Vegetables are an essential component of such a diet as they supply vitamins, minerals and fibre that are not found in any other food. In addition, doctors are recommending that we reduce the amount of animal fats and proteins we consume, so more and more people are experimenting with ways to cook vegetables, some to the point of excluding meat from their diets altogether.

The recipes in this book have been created with this food trend in mind. Many of them are substantial enough to be meals in themselves, especially those that contain the high protein pulses – dried beans, peas and lentils. Other recipes need only the addition of protein in the form of cheese, nuts or eggs to make them nutritionally complete. For non-vegetarians we give variations that suggest which type of meat, poultry or fish can be added – an excellent way of making a little meat go a long way.

Even if your family are great meat eaters it is a good idea to plan one vegetable-only meal a day. This may be a 'raw' salad or a mixture of cooked vegetables with perhaps some added cheese or nuts. This ensures your daily supply of vitamins and minerals, which are always best gained the natural way rather than from pills or tonics.

It is essential to buy really fresh vegetables and to prepare, cook and eat them as soon as possible, when their vitamin and mineral content is at its most potent.

The vitamin content of vegetables deteriorates with storage, so make an effort to buy from a supplier who stocks really fresh produce.

The general and all-important rule is to cook vegetables as briefly as possible. Cook them in as small an amount of water as possible until they are just tender. Most vegetables taste better if they are slightly undercooked and still crisp; moreover their vitamins and minerals will be preserved. There are a few exceptions, such as root vegetables and globe artichokes, but on the whole overcooked vegetables are spoilt vegetables.

Enjoy cooking vegetables and become familiar with some of the less well known varieties. Fortunately, modern methods of cultivation, preservation and transportation make it possible for a great selection of fresh vegetables to be available throughout the year. If, however, the vegetable required for a particular recipe is unavailable, try experimenting with a different one, creating new combinations of flavour. Try vegetables you have never eaten before, it is the only way to discover which of the unfamiliar vegetables you might like.

In most of the recipes that follow, fresh vegetables may be replaced by frozen, although anyone who is lucky enough to grow their own will know that nothing can compare with the flavour of really fresh vegetables.

Hopefully, the following recipes will inspire you to experiment with unfamiliar vegetables and to make more use of the old, old favourites, so that vegetables will play an even greater part in your cooking.

HOT AND COLD SOUPS

Soups are usually associated with the winter months but some of the following recipes can be served chilled, perfect for those lazy summer days. Many of the recipes require the use of a food processor or blender but you can use a sieve or food mill; the soup will be just as smooth although it will take a little longer to prepare.

Tomato and Stilton Soup

METRIC/IMPERIAL
50g/2 oz butter
2 tablespoons olive oil
2 medium onions,
  chopped
2 garlic cloves, chopped
2 celery sticks, chopped
1 carrot, chopped
450 g/1 lb tomatoes,
  peeled and chopped
1 × 400 g/14 oz can
  tomatoes
900 ml/1½ pints chicken
  stock or water
2 tablespoons tomato
  purée
1 teaspoon sugar
1 teaspoon dried oregano
1 teaspoon salt
150 ml/¼ pint red wine
freshly ground black
  pepper
To garnish:
300 ml/½ pint single
  cream (optional)
100 g/4 oz crumbled
  Stilton cheese
100 g/4 oz croûtons (see
  right)

AMERICAN
¼ cup butter
2 tablespoons olive oil
2 medium onions,
  chopped
2 garlic cloves, chopped
2 stalks celery, chopped
1 carrot, chopped
1 lb tomatoes, peeled and
  chopped
1 × 14 oz can tomatoes
3¾ cups chicken stock or
  water
2 tablespoons tomato
  paste
1 teaspoon sugar
1 teaspoon dried oregano
1 teaspoon salt
⅔ cup red wine
freshly ground black
  pepper
To garnish:
1¼ cups light cream
  (optional)
1 cup crumbled Stilton
  cheese
1 cup croûtons (see right)

Heat the butter and oil in a large saucepan and gently sauté the onion, garlic and celery until soft. Add the carrot and the fresh tomatoes and cook together for about 10 minutes, stirring occasionally. Add the canned tomatoes and the stock or water together with the tomato purée (paste), sugar, oregano, salt, wine and pepper. Bring to the boil, then reduce the heat and simmer for 1 hour.

Allow the soup to cool slightly, then transfer to a food processor or blender and process for about 1 minute, until smooth. If a finer-textured soup is preferred, process again for a further minute. Alternatively, press the soup through a sieve. Return the soup to the saucepan to reheat, taste and correct the seasoning, if necessary, and serve piping hot with a swirl of cream in each bowl, if liked. Garnish with a sprinkling of Stilton or croûtons, or both.
Serves 8

Croûtons: Cut slices of bread (crusts removed) into tiny cubes. Fry in oil or butter until golden and crisp and then drain on kitchen paper.

Tomato and Stilton Soup

Leek, Potato and Fennel Soup

METRIC/IMPERIAL	AMERICAN
50 g/2 oz butter	¼ cup butter
6 large leeks, sliced and thoroughly washed	6 large leeks, sliced and thoroughly washed
3 large potatoes, diced	3 large potatoes, diced
1 small head of fennel, chopped	1 small head of fennel, chopped
1.2 litres/2 pints vegetable stock or water	5 cups vegetable stock or water
1 teaspoon salt	1 teaspoon salt
½ teaspoon grated nutmeg	½ teaspoon grated nutmeg
½ teaspoon ground cumin	½ teaspoon ground cumin
250 ml/8 fl oz single cream	1 cup light cream
freshly ground black pepper	freshly ground black pepper
chopped fresh chives to garnish	chopped fresh chives to garnish

Melt the butter in a large saucepan over a low heat. Add the leeks, potatoes and fennel, cover and simmer for about 10 minutes, stirring occasionally. Add the stock or water, salt, nutmeg and cumin and simmer gently, covered, for 1 hour.

Allow the soup to cool slightly, then transfer to a food processor or a blender and process for about 1 minute until smooth. Add the cream and the pepper and process again. Taste and correct the seasoning if necessary. Heat up again when ready to serve or serve cold. Garnish with chopped chives.
Serves 12

Variation: Add 100 g/4 oz (½ cup) diced ham towards the end of the cooking time.

Minestrone

METRIC/IMPERIAL	AMERICAN
4 tablespoons olive oil	4 tablespoons olive oil
2 medium onions, sliced	2 medium onions, sliced
2 garlic cloves, chopped	2 garlic cloves, chopped
3 medium carrots, sliced	3 medium carrots, sliced
100 g/4 oz red kidney beans, soaked overnight and drained	⅔ cup red kidney beans, soaked overnight and drained
2 celery sticks, with leaves, sliced	2 stalks celery, with leaves, sliced
1 green pepper, cored, seeded and sliced	1 green pepper, cored, seeded and sliced
1 chilli, seeded and sliced	1 chili, seeded and sliced
1 parsnip, peeled and diced	1 parsnip, peeled and diced
2 potatoes, diced	2 potatoes, diced
1 medium head of fennel, chopped	1 medium head of fennel, chopped
100 g/4 oz cabbage, shredded	1½ cups shredded cabbage
1 tablespoon chopped fresh parsley	1 tablespoon chopped fresh parsley
1 tablespoon chopped fresh coriander	1 tablespoon chopped fresh coriander
2 litres/3½ pints stock or water	9 cups stock or water
2 teaspoons salt	2 teaspoons salt
2 bay leaves	2 bay leaves
1 teaspoon dried basil	1 teaspoon dried basil
1 teaspoon grated nutmeg	1 teaspoon grated nutmeg
freshly ground black pepper	freshly ground black pepper
dash of Tabasco sauce	dash of hot pepper sauce
1 × 350 g/12 oz can tomatoes	1 × 12 oz can tomatoes
100 g/4 oz pasta shells (optional)	1 cup pasta shells (optional)
50 g/2 oz grated Parmesan cheese	½ cup grated Parmesan cheese

Heat the oil in a large saucepan over a low heat and sauté the onions, garlic and carrots for about 5 minutes. Add the remaining vegetables and herbs, stir well, then add the stock or water and the salt, bay leaves, basil, nutmeg, pepper and Tabasco (hot pepper) sauce. Bring slowly to the boil and add the tomatoes. Reduce the heat and simmer for about 1½ hours. If desired, add the pasta about halfway through the cooking time. Remove the bay leaves and serve piping hot with Parmesan cheese sprinkled on the top.
Serves 12

Gazpacho

METRIC/IMPERIAL	AMERICAN
1 cucumber, peeled and sliced	1 cucumber, peeled and sliced
6 tomatoes, peeled and sliced	6 tomatoes, peeled and sliced
1 large onion, sliced	1 large onion, sliced
1 green pepper, cored, seeded and sliced	1 green pepper, cored, seeded and sliced
4 garlic cloves, sliced	4 garlic cloves, sliced
1 litre/1¾ pints tomato juice or water	4 cups tomato juice or water
120 ml/4 fl oz olive oil	½ cup olive oil
120 ml/4 fl oz wine vinegar	½ cup wine vinegar
grated rind and juice of 1 lemon	grated rind and juice of 1 lemon
1 teaspoon salt	1 teaspoon salt
freshly ground black pepper	freshly ground black pepper
dash of Tabasco sauce	dash of hot pepper sauce
100 g/4 oz fresh white breadcrumbs	2 cups soft white bread crumbs
To garnish:	**To garnish:**
2 tablespoons chopped cucumber	2 tablespoons chopped cucumber
2 tablespoons chopped tomatoes	2 tablespoons chopped tomatoes
2 tablespoons chopped onion	2 tablespoons chopped onion
2 tablespoons chopped green pepper	2 tablespoons chopped green pepper
2 tablespoons chopped fresh parsley	2 tablespoons chopped fresh parsley
4 tablespoons croûtons (see page 7)	4 tablespoons croûtons (see page 7)

Place the vegetables in a food processor or blender with the tomato juice or water and process for 1 minute. Add the oil, vinegar, lemon rind and juice, salt, pepper, Tabasco (hot pepper) sauce and the breadcrumbs, and process again for a further 1 minute.

Transfer the soup to a bowl and chill thoroughly in the refrigerator for at least 3 hours. Serve cold with a plate of chopped cucumber, tomato, onion, green pepper, parsley and croûtons to garnish.

Serves 8

Pumpkin and Ginger Soup

METRIC/IMPERIAL	AMERICAN
2.5 cm/1 inch ginger root, scrubbed	1 inch ginger root, scrubbed
2 garlic cloves	2 garlic cloves
2 tablespoons vegetable oil	2 tablespoons vegetable oil
¼ large pumpkin, peeled and diced	¼ large pumpkin, peeled and diced
2 medium onions, chopped	2 medium onions, chopped
2 celery sticks, sliced	2 stalks celery, sliced
1 green pepper, cored, seeded and sliced	1 green pepper, cored, seeded and sliced
1 chilli, seeded and sliced	1 chili, seeded and sliced
1.2 litres/2 pints chicken stock or water	5 cups chicken stock or water
1 teaspoon ground coriander	1 teaspoon ground coriander
1 teaspoon ground cumin	1 teaspoon ground cumin
1 teaspoon dried basil	1 teaspoon dried basil
1 teaspoon mixed spice	1 teaspoon ground allspice
2 bay leaves	2 bay leaves
dash of Tabasco sauce	dash of hot pepper sauce
salt	salt
freshly ground black pepper	freshly ground black pepper

Place the ginger, garlic and oil in a food processor or blender and process for 1 minute. Place all the ingredients in a large saucepan or a pressure cooker. Bring to the boil, then reduce the heat and simmer for 1½ hours. If using a pressure cooker, bring to high pressure and cook for 10 minutes.

Allow the soup to cool slightly, then remove the bay leaves and transfer the soup to a food processor or blender and process for about 1 minute until smooth. Alternatively, put the soup through a food mill or pass through a sieve. Return the soup to the saucepan to reheat, taste and correct the seasoning if necessary, and serve piping hot.

Serves 8

Spicy Borsch

METRIC/IMPERIAL	AMERICAN
100 g/4 oz butter	½ cup butter
750 g/1½ lb raw beetroot, grated	6 cups grated raw beet
¼ red cabbage, chopped	¼ red cabbage, chopped
2 large potatoes, diced	2 large potatoes, diced
3 medium onions, sliced	3 medium onions, sliced
2 celery sticks, sliced	2 stalks celery, sliced
1 carrot, grated	1 carrot, grated
1.2 litres/2 pints stock or water	5 cups stock or water
2.5 cm/1 inch ginger root, grated	1 inch ginger root, grated
2 garlic cloves, crushed	2 garlic cloves, crushed
6 peppercorns	6 peppercorns
3 cloves	3 cloves
2 tablespoons vinegar	2 tablespoons vinegar
1 teaspoon grated nutmeg	1 teaspoon grated nutmeg
1 teaspoon mixed spice	1 teaspoon ground allspice
1 teaspoon ground coriander	1 teaspoon ground coriander
1 teaspoon ground cumin	1 teaspoon ground cumin
1 teaspoon salt	1 teaspoon salt
250 ml/8 fl oz soured cream (optional)	1 cup sour cream (optional)
single cream to garnish (optional)	light cream to garnish (optional)

Melt the butter in a pressure cooker or large saucepan over a low heat. Add all the vegetables and cook slowly together for about 10 minutes. Add the stock or water and the ginger, garlic, peppercorns, cloves, vinegar, spices and salt. Bring to the boil or to high pressure, then simmer for 1½ hours or cook at high pressure for 10 minutes.

Allow the soup to cool slightly and remove the peppercorns and cloves. Transfer to a food processor or blender and process for about 1 minute, until smooth. Alternatively, press the soup through a sieve. Taste and correct the seasoning, if necessary, and add the soured cream if desired. Serve hot or cold with a little single (light) cream swirled into each bowl, if desired.
Serves 12

Candied Onion Soup

METRIC/IMPERIAL	AMERICAN
100 g/4 oz butter	½ cup butter
750 g/1½ lb onions, sliced	5 cups sliced onions
1 garlic clove, chopped	1 garlic clove, chopped
1 teaspoon brown sugar	1 teaspoon brown sugar
2 teaspoons salt	2 teaspoons salt
1.75 litres/3 pints duck stock or water	7½ cups duck stock or water
2 bay leaves	2 bay leaves
4 tablespoons sherry	¼ cup sherry
8 slices French bread, buttered	8 slices French bread, buttered
8 teaspoons grated Parmesan cheese	8 teaspoons grated Parmesan cheese

Melt the butter in a large saucepan over a low heat. Add the onions and garlic. Raise the heat slightly and cook, covered, for about 10 minutes. Add the sugar and the salt and cook for a further 10 minutes, stirring occasionally, until brown. Add the stock or water, bay leaves and sherry, and bring to the boil. Reduce the heat and simmer for 45 minutes.

Meanwhile, place the bread on a baking sheet and sprinkle each slice with 1 teaspoon Parmesan cheese. Bake in a preheated moderately hot oven (190°C/375°F, Gas Mark 5) for 15 minutes or until nicely browned.

Remove the bay leaves from the soup and serve piping hot, adding a slice of toasted cheese to each bowl.
Serves 8

Candied Onion Soup
Spicy Borsch

Cucumber and Potato Soup

METRIC/IMPERIAL	AMERICAN
50 g/2 oz butter	¼ cup butter
1 cucumber, peeled and sliced	1 cucumber, peeled and sliced
1 medium onion, sliced	1 medium onion, sliced
2 garlic cloves, chopped	2 garlic cloves, chopped
2 medium potatoes, diced	2 medium potatoes, diced
1 litre/1¾ pints chicken stock or water	4 cups chicken stock or water
1 teaspoon salt	1 teaspoon salt
freshly ground black pepper	freshly ground black pepper
120 ml/4 fl oz single cream or milk	½ cup light cream or milk

Melt the butter in a large saucepan over a low heat. Add the cucumber, onion, garlic and potato, cover and cook for 10 minutes. Add the stock or water and the salt and pepper and bring to the boil. Reduce the heat and simmer for 30 minutes.

Allow the soup to cool slightly, then transfer to a food processor or blender and process for about 1 minute, until smooth. Alternatively, press the soup through a sieve. Add the cream or milk and stir well, or process again briefly. Taste and correct the seasoning if necessary, and add more milk or cream, if desired. Serve cold.
Serves 6

Cream of Asparagus Soup

METRIC/IMPERIAL	AMERICAN
50 g/2 oz butter	¼ cup butter
450 g/1 lb asparagus, trimmed and chopped	1 lb asparagus, trimmed and chopped
2 onions, chopped	2 onions, chopped
1 lettuce heart, chopped	1 lettuce heart, chopped
600 ml/1 pint chicken stock or water	2½ cups chicken stock or water
600 ml/1 pint milk	2½ cups milk
1 large potato, diced	1 large potato, diced
1 teaspoon salt	1 teaspoon salt
1 tablespoon chopped fresh basil	1 tablespoon chopped fresh basil
1 bouquet garni	1 bouquet garni
120 ml/4 fl oz single cream	½ cup light cream

Melt the butter in a large saucepan over a low heat and add the asparagus, onions and lettuce. Sauté for about 10 minutes, then add the stock or water, milk and potato. Stir well, and add the salt, basil and bouquet garni. Bring to the boil, reduce the heat and simmer for 1 hour.

At the end of the cooking time, remove the bouquet garni, add the cream and allow the soup to cool slightly. Transfer to a food processor or blender and process for about 1 minute, until smooth. Alternatively, press the soup through a sieve. Return the soup to the saucepan to reheat and serve piping hot, or serve cold.
Serves 8

Curried Carrot Soup

METRIC/IMPERIAL	AMERICAN
50 g/2 oz butter	¼ cup butter
1 medium onion, sliced	1 medium onion, sliced
2 garlic cloves, chopped	2 garlic cloves, chopped
750 g/1½ lb carrots, grated	6 cups grated carrot
1.2 litres/2 pints chicken stock or water	5 cups chicken stock or water
2.5 cm/1 inch ginger root, grated	1 inch ginger root, grated
1 teaspoon curry powder	1 teaspoon curry powder
½ teaspoon grated nutmeg	½ teaspoon grated nutmeg
½ teaspoon salt	½ teaspoon salt
250 ml/8 fl oz single cream	1 cup light cream
freshly ground black pepper	freshly ground black pepper
2 tablespoons chopped fresh parsley to garnish	2 tablespoons chopped fresh parsley to garnish

Melt the butter in a large saucepan over a low heat. Add the onion and the garlic and sauté gently for a few minutes. Add the grated carrot, stir well, cover and sweat for 10 minutes. Add the stock or water and bring to the boil. Reduce the heat and add the ginger, curry powder, nutmeg and salt. Simmer for 30 minutes, then add the cream. Place in a food processor or blender and process for about 1 minute. Add the pepper, taste and correct the seasoning if necessary. Process again briefly. Serve hot or cold, garnished with chopped parsley.
Serves 12

Variation: For slimmers, replace the cream with skimmed milk or half and half.

Three Bean Soup

METRIC/IMPERIAL	AMERICAN
225 g/8 oz dried red kidney beans	1⅓ cups dried red kidney beans
225 g/8 oz dried butter beans	1⅓ cups dried butter beans
225 g/8 oz dried black-eye beans	1⅓ cups dried black-eye beans
225 g/8 oz cracked wheat	1¾ cups cracked wheat
50 g/2 oz butter	¼ cup butter
2 medium onions, sliced	2 medium onions, sliced
1 garlic clove, chopped	1 garlic clove, chopped
2 celery sticks, sliced	2 stalks celery, sliced
1.75 litres/3 pints chicken stock or water	7½ cups chicken stock or water
2 teaspoons salt	2 teaspoons salt
1 teaspoon grated nutmeg	1 teaspoon grated nutmeg
1 teaspoon mixed spice	1 teaspoon ground allspice
2 bay leaves	2 bay leaves
1 teaspoon dried basil	1 teaspoon dried basil
grated rind and juice of 1 lemon	grated rind and juice of 1 lemon
8 tablespoons croûtons (see page 7) to garnish (optional)	8 tablespoons croûtons (see page 7) to garnish (optional)

Place the beans and the cracked wheat in two large bowls, cover with cold water and leave to soak overnight. Next day, change the water and drain again just before using.

Melt the butter in a large saucepan over a low heat and gently sauté the onions, garlic and celery. Drain the soaked beans and cracked wheat and stir in thoroughly. Add the stock or water, salt, spices, herbs, lemon rind and juice. Bring to the boil, cover and simmer gently for about 2 hours or until the beans are thoroughly soft. Alternatively, this soup can be cooked in a pressure cooker at high pressure for 20 minutes and allowed to cool at room temperature. Remove the bay leaves and serve piping hot with croûtons, if liked.
Serves 8

Note: This soup is not for slimmers as it contains approximately 400 calories (1680 kilojoules) per serving.

Split Pea and Almond Soup

METRIC/IMPERIAL	AMERICAN
50 g/2 oz butter	¼ cup butter
2 tablespoons olive oil	2 tablespoons olive oil
2 medium onions, sliced	2 medium onions, sliced
2 garlic cloves, chopped	2 garlic cloves, chopped
2 celery sticks, with leaves, chopped	2 stalks celery, with leaves, chopped
1 carrot, sliced	1 carrot, sliced
450 g/1 lb split peas	2 cups split peas
1.75 litres/3 pints ham stock or water	7½ cups ham stock or water
1 teaspoon grated nutmeg	1 teaspoon grated nutmeg
1 teaspoon ground cumin	1 teaspoon ground cumin
1 teaspoon ground coriander	1 teaspoon ground coriander
1 teaspoon salt (see method)	1 teaspoon salt (see method)
To garnish:	**To garnish:**
50 g/2 oz flaked almonds, toasted	¼ cup slivered almonds, toasted
1 tablespoon chopped fresh parsley	1 tablespoon chopped fresh parsley

Heat the butter and oil in a large saucepan over a low heat. Gently sauté the onions, garlic, celery and carrot for about 10 minutes until soft. Add the split peas, stock or water, nutmeg, cumin and coriander. Add salt only after tasting the soup; if the stock used was salty it may not be needed. Bring to the boil and simmer gently for 1½ hours, stirring occasionally.

The soup can be served immediately, but if a puréed soup is preferred, allow the soup to cool slightly, then transfer to a food processor or blender and process for about 1 minute until smooth. Correct the seasoning and process again for a further minute, if necessary. Return the soup to the saucepan to reheat and serve piping hot, garnished with toasted almonds and chopped parsley.
Serves 12

Variation: Add 100 g/4 oz (½ cup) chopped ham.

Green Pea and Lettuce Soup

METRIC/IMPERIAL	AMERICAN
100 g/4 oz butter	½ cup butter
450 g/1 lb shelled fresh or frozen peas	3 cups shelled fresh or frozen peas
2 lettuce hearts, chopped	2 lettuce hearts, chopped
1.2 litres/2 pints ham stock or water	5 cups ham stock or water
1 teaspoon salt	1 teaspoon salt
1 teaspoon dried basil	1 teaspoon dried basil
1 teaspoon grated nutmeg	1 teaspoon grated nutmeg
2 bay leaves	2 bay leaves
To garnish:	**To garnish:**
120 ml/4 fl oz single cream	½ cup light cream
2 tablespoons chopped fresh parsley	2 tablespoons chopped fresh parsley

Melt the butter in a large saucepan over a low heat. Add the peas, straight from the freezer if you are using frozen. Add the chopped lettuce, cover the saucepan and sweat for 10 minutes. Add the stock or water, salt, basil, nutmeg and bay leaves and bring to the boil. Reduce the heat and simmer for 40 minutes.

Allow the soup to cool slightly, then remove the bay leaves and transfer the soup to a food processor or blender and process for about 1 minute. Taste and correct the seasoning, if necessary, and process again briefly. Reheat the soup and serve piping hot, garnished with a swirl of cream and a pinch of parsley. *Serves 8*

Variation: Add 100 g/4 oz (½ cup) chopped ham at the end of the cooking time.

Cream of Mushroom Soup

METRIC/IMPERIAL	AMERICAN
50 g/2 oz butter	¼ cup butter
1 medium onion, sliced	1 medium onion, sliced
2 garlic cloves, chopped	2 garlic cloves, chopped
450 g/1 lb mushrooms, sliced (preferably flat)	4 cups sliced mushrooms (preferably flat)
1 tablespoon chopped fresh parsley	1 tablespoon chopped fresh parsley
1 litre/1¾ pints chicken stock or water	4 cups chicken stock or water
250 ml/8 fl oz single cream	1 cup light cream
1 teaspoon salt	1 teaspoon salt
freshly ground black pepper	freshly ground black pepper

Melt the butter in a large saucepan over a low heat. Add the onion and garlic and sauté gently for 1 to 2 minutes.

Add the mushrooms, cover loosely and cook for 10 minutes. Add the parsley and the stock or water. Bring to the boil, then reduce the heat and simmer for 20 minutes. Add the cream and the salt and pepper and heat for a further 5 minutes without boiling.

Allow the soup to cool slightly, then transfer to a food processor or blender and process until smooth. Alternatively, put the soup through a food mill or press through a sieve. Serve immediately. *Serves 8*

Hot Lentil Soup

METRIC/IMPERIAL	AMERICAN
450 g/1 lb red lentils, rinsed	1 lb red lentils, rinsed
50 g/2 oz butter	¼ cup butter
2 medium onions, chopped	2 medium onions, chopped
2 garlic cloves, chopped	2 garlic cloves, chopped
2 celery sticks, chopped	2 stalks celery, chopped
1 × 400 g/14 oz can tomatoes	1 × 14 oz can tomatoes
1 chilli, seeded and chopped (optional)	1 chili, seeded and chopped (optional)
1 teaspoon paprika	1 teaspoon paprika
1 teaspoon chilli powder	1 teaspoon chili powder
1 teaspoon ground cumin	1 teaspoon ground cumin
1 teaspoon salt	1 teaspoon salt
freshly ground black pepper	freshly ground black pepper
1.2 litres/2 pints chicken stock or water	5 cups chicken stock or water

Place the lentils in a bowl of water, picking out any discoloured ones or stones. Meanwhile, melt the butter in a large saucepan over low heat and sauté the onions, garlic and celery until softened.

Drain the lentils and add them to the vegetables with the tomatoes. Stir well to combine. Add the remaining ingredients, cover and simmer gently for about 2 hours. Add a little more water if the soup becomes too thick and be careful not to burn the bottom. Served hot with wholewheat toast, this soup is a meal in itself. *Serves 8*

Variation: Add any leftover meat, such as chicken or beef.

Hot Lentil Soup
Green Pea and Lettuce Soup

Parsnip and Peanut Butter Soup

METRIC/IMPERIAL	AMERICAN
50 g/2 oz butter	¼ cup butter
1 medium onion, sliced	1 medium onion, sliced
2 garlic cloves, chopped	2 garlic cloves, chopped
5 medium parsnips, peeled and chopped	5 medium parsnips, peeled and chopped
1.2 litres/2 pints chicken stock or water	5 cups chicken stock or water
100 g/4 oz peanut butter	½ cup peanut butter
1 teaspoon salt	1 teaspoon salt
1 teaspoon grated nutmeg	1 teaspoon grated nutmeg
2 bay leaves	2 bay leaves
freshly ground black pepper	freshly ground black pepper
2 tablespoons salted peanuts to garnish	2 tablespoons salted peanuts to garnish

Melt the butter in a large saucepan over a low heat. A pressure cooker can be used. Add the onion and garlic, cook for a few minutes, then add the chopped parsnips. Cover and sweat for about 10 minutes. Add the stock or water, the peanut butter and the salt, nutmeg, bay leaves and pepper. Bring to the boil, then reduce the heat and simmer gently for 45 minutes. If using a pressure cooker, bring to high pressure and cook for 7 minutes. Remove from the heat and allow the pressure to decrease at room temperature.

Allow the soup to cool slightly, then remove the bay leaves and transfer the soup to a food processor or blender and process for about 1 minute until smooth. Correct the seasoning and process again briefly. Return the soup to the saucepan, reheat and serve piping hot, garnished with peanuts.
Serves 8

Spinach and Apple Soup

METRIC/IMPERIAL	AMERICAN
50 g/2 oz butter	¼ cup butter
1 kg/2 lb spinach with stalks, washed	2 lb spinach with stalks, washed
1 medium onion, chopped	1 medium onion, chopped
2 dessert apples, cored, peeled and sliced	2 dessert apples, cored, peeled and sliced
1 large potato, chopped	1 large potato, chopped
1.2 litres/2 pints chicken stock or water	5 cups chicken stock or water
1 teaspoon salt	1 teaspoon salt
1 teaspoon grated nutmeg	1 teaspoon grated nutmeg
freshly ground black pepper	freshly ground black pepper
single cream to garnish	light cream to garnish

Melt the butter in a large saucepan over a low heat and add the wet spinach. Cook over a moderate heat, turning constantly, until the spinach is reduced in size and partially cooked. Roughly chop the spinach in the saucepan and add the remaining ingredients, except the cream. Simmer gently for about 45 minutes.

Allow the soup to cool slightly, then transfer to a food processor or blender and process for about 1 minute, until smooth. Alternatively, press the soup through a sieve. Serve hot or cold, garnished with cream.
Serves 12

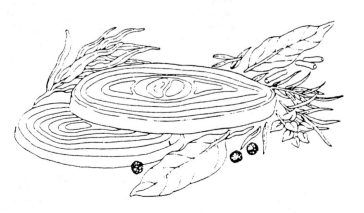

Artichoke and Celery Soup

METRIC/IMPERIAL	AMERICAN
450 g/1 lb Jerusalem artichokes	1 lb Jerusalem artichokes
2 tablespoons vinegar	2 tablespoons vinegar
50 g/2 oz butter	¼ cup butter
1 medium onion, chopped	1 medium onion, chopped
2 celery sticks, chopped	2 stalks celery, chopped
600 ml/1 pint milk	2½ cups milk
600 ml/1 pint chicken stock or water	2½ cups chicken stock or water
1 teaspoon salt	1 teaspoon salt
1 teaspoon grated nutmeg	1 teaspoon grated nutmeg
freshly ground black pepper	freshly ground black pepper
wholewheat croûtons (see page 7) to garnish	wholewheat croûtons (see page 7) to garnish

Peel and chop the artichokes and place them in a bowl of water with the vinegar to prevent discoloration. Melt the butter in a large saucepan over a low heat and gently sauté the onion and the celery until soft.

Drain the artichokes and add them to the saucepan. Add the remaining ingredients. Bring to the boil, reduce the heat and simmer gently for about 1 hour.

Allow the soup to cool slightly, then transfer to a food processor or blender and process for about 1 minute, until smooth. Alternatively, press the soup through a sieve. Return the soup to the saucepan to reheat, taste and correct the seasoning, if necessary, and serve piping hot with croûtons.
Serves 8

Cauliflower and Parmesan Soup

METRIC/IMPERIAL	AMERICAN
50 g/2 oz butter	¼ cup butter
1 cauliflower, including leaves, chopped	1 cauliflower, including leaves, chopped
2 leeks, sliced and thoroughly washed	2 leeks, sliced and thoroughly washed
2 garlic cloves, chopped	2 garlic cloves, chopped
1 large potato, diced	1 large potato, diced
600 ml/1 pint milk	2½ cups milk
600 ml/1 pint chicken stock or water	2½ cups chicken stock or water
1 teaspoon grated nutmeg	1 teaspoon grated nutmeg
1 teaspoon salt	1 teaspoon salt
2 tablespoons Parmesan cheese to garnish	2 tablespoons Parmesan cheese to garnish

Melt the butter in a large saucepan over a low heat. Add the cauliflower, leeks, garlic and potato and sauté for 5 minutes, stirring occasionally. Add the milk and the stock or water with the nutmeg and salt and gently bring to the boil. Reduce the heat and simmer for 45 minutes.

Allow the soup to cool slightly, then transfer to a food processor or blender and process for about 1 minute until smooth. If a finer purée is required, process for another minute. Return the soup to the saucepan to reheat and serve piping hot, garnished with Parmesan cheese.
Serves 8

Variation: Crumble crisp-fried bacon on top of the Parmesan cheese.

Watercress Soup

METRIC/IMPERIAL	AMERICAN
50 g/2 oz butter	¼ cup butter
1 medium onion, sliced	1 medium onion, sliced
2 garlic cloves, chopped	2 garlic cloves, chopped
1 medium potato, diced	1 medium potato, diced
2 bunches watercress, chopped	2 bunches watercress, chopped
1 litre/1¾ pints chicken stock or water	4 cups chicken stock or water
1 teaspoon salt	1 teaspoon salt
freshly ground black pepper	freshly ground black pepper
1 bay leaf	1 bay leaf
120 ml/4 fl oz single cream or milk	½ cup light cream or milk
8 tablespoons croûtons (see page 7) to garnish (optional)	8 tablespoons croûtons (see page 7) to garnish (optional)

Melt the butter in a large saucepan over a low heat. Add the onion, garlic and potato and cook gently for about 5 minutes. Add the watercress, including the stalks, and stir thoroughly. Add the stock or water, salt, pepper and bay leaf. Bring to the boil, then reduce the heat and simmer gently for 30 minutes.

Allow the soup to cool slightly, then remove the bay leaf and transfer the soup to a food processor or blender. Process for about 1 minute, until smooth. Alternatively, press the soup through a sieve. Add the cream or milk and stir well, or process again briefly, and leave to cool. Serve cold, sprinkling each portion with 1 tablespoon croûtons, if liked.
Serves 8

Variation: Sprinkle over crumbled crisp-fried bacon.

SIMPLE STARTERS

Light vegetable starters are perfect to serve at a dinner party. Most are quick and inexpensive to create and many are low in calories. It would be a shame, however, to restrict some of these recipes to the beginning of a meal, many of the more substantial starters make appetizing light meals especially if accompanied by a salad.

Spinach and Ricotta Puffs

METRIC/IMPERIAL	AMERICAN
750 g/1½ lb spinach, washed and stalks removed or 350 g/12 oz frozen spinach	1½ lb spinach, washed and stalks removed or 12 oz frozen spinach
350 g/12 oz Ricotta cheese	1½ cups Ricotta cheese
150 ml/¼ pint plain yogurt	⅔ cup plain yogurt
2 tablespoons chopped fresh chives	2 tablespoons chopped fresh chives
½ teaspoon salt	½ teaspoon salt
freshly ground black pepper	freshly ground black pepper
½ teaspoon grated nutmeg	½ teaspoon grated nutmeg
350 g/12 oz filo pastry (see Note)	¾ lb filo pastry (see Note)
100 g/4 oz unsalted butter, melted	½ cup unsalted butter, melted
1 bunch watercress to garnish	1 bunch watercress to garnish

Cook the spinach in a very little boiling salted water for about 7 minutes, until just tender. If using frozen spinach, cook it according to the instructions on the packet. Drain thoroughly, chop finely and leave to cool. Combine the Ricotta with the yogurt, chives, salt, pepper and nutmeg, add the cold spinach and mix well.

Place the filo pastry on a board and cut into 10 cm/ 4 inch strips, cutting through all the sheets at once. Cover with a clean damp cloth to keep the pastry moist while making up the puffs. Take one strip of pastry and brush with melted butter. Place 1 teaspoon of the spinach and cheese mixture at one end of the strip and fold over diagonally to make a triangular parcel. Continue with the remaining pastry and spinach mixture until you have made about 40 puffs. Arrange on baking sheets (about 10 puffs on each) and brush with melted butter. Bake in a preheated moderately hot oven (200°C/400°F, Gas Mark 6) for about 12 minutes, until nicely browned. Cool on a wire rack before serving garnished with watercress.
Makes 40
Note: Filo pastry is available from delicatessens and Greek food shops, but puff or flaky pastry rolled very thinly produces good results.

Avocado, Tomato and Smoked Mackerel

METRIC/IMPERIAL	AMERICAN
1 large avocado, stoned, peeled and sliced	1 large avocado, pitted, peeled and sliced
1 large tomato, sliced	1 large tomato, sliced
1 large fillet smoked mackerel, chopped	1 large filet smoked mackerel, chopped
1 tablespoon olive oil	1 tablespoon olive oil
2 tablespoons lemon juice	2 tablespoons lemon juice
½ teaspoon salt	½ teaspoon salt
freshly ground black pepper	freshly ground black pepper
wholewheat toast to serve	wholewheat toast to serve

In a large bowl, combine the avocado, tomato and mackerel. Add the olive oil, lemon juice and salt and pepper to taste. Stir until thoroughly combined or transfer to a food processor or blender and process very briefly. The mixture should retain its texture and not be a purée. Serve with hot wholewheat toast.
Serves 6

Spinach and Ricotta Puffs

Courgette (Zucchini) and Carrot Pancakes

METRIC/IMPERIAL
Pancakes:
100 g/4 oz wholewheat
  flour
½ teaspoon salt
1 egg
1 egg yolk
250 ml/8 fl oz milk
vegetable oil for frying
single cream to garnish
Filling:
2 courgettes, grated
1 carrot, grated
100 g/4 oz cream cheese
2 tablespoons chopped
  fresh chives
salt
freshly ground black
  pepper

AMERICAN
Pancakes:
1 cup wholewheat flour
½ teaspoon salt
1 egg
1 egg yolk
1 cup milk
vegetable oil for frying
light cream to garnish
Filling:
2 zucchini, grated
1 carrot, grated
½ cup cream cheese
2 tablespoons chopped
  fresh chives
salt
freshly ground black
  pepper

To make the pancake batter, combine the flour and salt in a bowl and make a well in the centre. Add the egg and the egg yolk and whisk, adding the milk gradually and slowly whisking in the flour. Whisk until smooth, then leave in the refrigerator for 1 hour. Meanwhile, prepare the filling by combining all the ingredients in a bowl.

Heat a very little oil in a small frying pan (skillet) or special pancake pan. Pour in just enough pancake batter to cover the bottom of the pan and cook gently until the underside is golden brown. Turn the pancake and cook the other side for a few seconds. Place about 2 teaspoons of the vegetable filling on the pancake, roll it up and transfer to an ovenproof dish. Continue making and filling the pancakes until you have 12.

Just before serving, pour a little cream over the pancakes and place in a moderately hot oven (190°C/375°F, Gas Mark 5) for 10 minutes, until warmed through.
Serves 6

Mushroom Crêpes

METRIC/IMPERIAL
Crêpes:
100 g/4 oz plain flour
½ teaspoon salt
1 egg
1 egg yolk
250 ml/8 fl oz milk
vegetable oil for frying
Filling:
50 g/2 oz butter
3 field mushrooms or
  cèpes, chopped
1 medium onion,
  chopped
3 garlic cloves, crushed
1 tablespoon chopped
  fresh parsley
1 teaspoon wholewheat
  flour
salt
freshly ground black
  pepper
To garnish:
grated Parmesan cheese

AMERICAN
Crêpes:
1 cup all-purpose flour
½ teaspoon salt
1 egg
1 egg yolk
1 cup milk
vegetable oil for frying
Filling:
¼ cup butter
3 field mushrooms or
  cèpes, chopped
1 medium onion,
  chopped
3 garlic cloves, crushed
1 tablespoon chopped
  fresh parsley
1 teaspoon wholewheat
  flour
salt
freshly ground black
  pepper
To garnish:
grated Parmesan cheese

To make the crêpe batter, sift the flour and salt together in a bowl. Make a well in the centre and add the egg and egg yolk. Whisk from the centre, gradually adding the milk and whisking in the flour. Continue whisking until smooth, then leave in the refrigerator for 1 hour.

Meanwhile, make the filling. Melt the butter in a frying pan (skillet) and sauté the mushrooms, onion, garlic and parsley for about 15 minutes. Sprinkle over the flour, add salt and pepper and cook for a further 1 to 2 minutes. Remove from the heat and keep warm.

Heat a very little oil in a 15 cm/6 inch frying pan (skillet) or special crêpe pan and pour in just enough batter to cover the bottom of the pan. Cook gently for 1 to 2 minutes until the underside is golden brown, then turn and cook the other side for 30 seconds. Place a little of the mushroom filling on the crêpe, roll it up, transfer to an ovenproof dish and keep warm. Continue making and filling the crêpes until you have made 12. Serve sprinkled with Parmesan cheese.
Serves 6

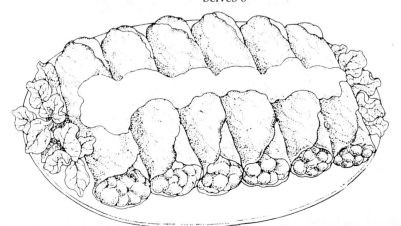

Olive and Mushroom Pâté

METRIC/IMPERIAL	AMERICAN
2 tablespoons olive oil	2 tablespoons olive oil
1 medium onion, chopped	1 medium onion, chopped
1 garlic clove, chopped	1 garlic clove, chopped
225 g/8 oz flat mushrooms, sliced	½ lb flat mushrooms, sliced
12 black olives, stoned	12 pitted ripe olives
1 tablespoon lemon juice	1 tablespoon lemon juice
1 tablespoon capers (optional)	1 tablespoon capers (optional)
salt	salt
freshly ground black pepper	freshly ground black pepper
1 tablespoon chopped fresh parsley to garnish	1 tablespoon chopped fresh parsley to garnish

Heat the oil in a frying pan (skillet) and gently sauté the onion and garlic until just translucent. Add the mushrooms and cook together for about 20 minutes, stirring occasionally. Add all the remaining ingredients, except the parsley, and combine well together.

Allow to cool slightly, then transfer to a food processor or blender and process briefly so that the pâté still has texture. Spoon into individual ramekin dishes, garnish with parsley and serve with hot wholewheat toast.
Serves 8

Note: This starter improves with age and is best made the day before and stored in the refrigerator overnight.

Coffee Marinated Mushrooms and Apricots

METRIC/IMPERIAL	AMERICAN
100 g/4 oz dried apricots	⅔ cup dried apricots
1 lemon, halved	1 lemon, halved
225 g/8 oz button mushrooms, trimmed	2 cups button mushrooms, trimmed
250 ml/8 fl oz strong black coffee	1 cup strong black coffee
120 ml/4 fl oz wine vinegar	½ cup wine vinegar
2 garlic cloves, crushed	2 garlic cloves, crushed
2 tablespoons chopped fresh coriander to garnish	2 tablespoons chopped fresh coriander to garnish

Place the apricots in a heatproof bowl and cover with boiling water. Squeeze the juice from one half of the lemon and add it, with the squeezed shell, to the bowl. Leave the apricots for 10 minutes until plump, then drain and discard the lemon shell.

Meanwhile, place the mushrooms in a large saucepan and cover with boiling water. Squeeze the remaining lemon half and add the juice and shell and blanch for 5 minutes. Drain the mushrooms and leave to cool, discarding the lemon shell.

To prepare the marinade, combine all the remaining ingredients, except the coriander, and whisk briefly. Add the apricots and mushrooms, stir thoroughly and leave to marinate for at least 3 to 4 hours, preferably overnight.

Drain the mushrooms and apricots and serve on individual plates with a little of the marinade. Garnish with coriander.
Serves 8

Vegetable Compote

METRIC/IMPERIAL	AMERICAN
225 g/8 oz tiny new potatoes	½ lb tiny new potatoes
225 g/8 oz tiny new carrots	½ lb tiny new carrots
1 bunch mint	1 bunch mint
juice of 1 lemon	juice of 1 lemon
1 small cauliflower	1 small cauliflower
100 g/4 oz shelled new garden peas	¾ cup shelled new garden peas
250 ml/8 fl oz mayonnaise	1 cup mayonnaise
2 garlic cloves, crushed	2 garlic cloves, crushed
salt	salt
freshly ground black pepper	freshly ground black pepper
2 tablespoons chopped fresh parsley to garnish	2 tablespoons chopped fresh parsley to garnish

Gently wash the potatoes and carrots; do not scrub them as the skins are delicious and help preserve the vitamins. Cook the potatoes and carrots separately in boiling salted water with a sprig of mint added until just tender. The potatoes will take about 7 minutes and the carrots about 5 minutes, depending on size. Drain, set aside and sprinkle with a little lemon juice to prevent them drying.

Break the cauliflower into florets and cook in boiling salted water for about 6 minutes until just tender. Drain, set aside and sprinkle with lemon juice. Cook the peas in the same way for about 5 minutes, until just tender, then drain. Combine all the vegetables.

Place the mayonnaise in a large bowl, add the garlic, remaining lemon juice, salt and pepper and mix well. Just before serving, combine the vegetables with the mayonnaise mixture and serve at once in individual ramekin dishes or on a large serving platter. Garnish with chopped parsley and sprigs of mint.
Serves 8

Variation: Top with a combination of diced chicken and ham.

Stuffed Tomatoes

METRIC/IMPERIAL	AMERICAN
4 large tomatoes	4 large tomatoes
50 g/2 oz fresh white breadcrumbs	1 cup soft white bread crumbs
1 green dessert apple, cored and chopped	1 green dessert apple, cored and chopped
1 tablespoon lemon juice	1 tablespoon lemon juice
100 g/4 oz finely grated Edam cheese	1 cup finely grated Edam cheese
75 g/3 oz chopped garlic sausage	½ cup chopped garlic sausage
1 teaspoon French mustard	1 teaspoon Dijon-style mustard
1 tablespoon chopped fresh basil	1 tablespoon chopped fresh basil
salt	salt
freshly ground black pepper	freshly ground black pepper
watercress to garnish	watercress to garnish

Cut a slice off the top of each tomato and reserve. Scoop out the seeds and pulp, chop finely and place in a bowl. Add all the remaining ingredients, except the watercress, mix well and pile into the tomato shells. Replace the tops and place in a greased ovenproof dish. Bake in a preheated moderately hot oven (190°C/375°F, Gas Mark 5) for 20 minutes, until the tomatoes are just tender. Garnish with watercress.
Serves 4

Guacamole

METRIC/IMPERIAL	AMERICAN
3 ripe avocados, stoned, peeled and chopped	3 ripe avocados, pitted, peeled and chopped
juice of 1 lemon	juice of 1 lemon
1 large tomato, peeled and chopped	1 large tomato, peeled and chopped
2 garlic cloves, crushed	2 garlic cloves, crushed
1 teaspoon paprika	1 teaspoon paprika
1 tablespoon olive oil	1 tablespoon olive oil
dash of Tabasco sauce	dash of hot pepper sauce
1 tablespoon wine vinegar	1 tablespoon wine vinegar
salt	salt
freshly ground black pepper	freshly ground black pepper
tortilla chips to serve	tortilla chips to serve

Do not make Guacamole too far ahead of time as it discolours very easily. Combine all the ingredients in a food processor or blender and process for about 1 minute, until smooth. Pile into a bowl or individual ramekin dishes and serve with corn chips.
Serves 8

Stuffed Aubergines (Eggplants)

METRIC/IMPERIAL	AMERICAN
4 aubergines, halved lengthwise	4 eggplants, halved lengthwise
2 tablespoons olive oil	2 tablespoons olive oil
1 medium onion, finely chopped	1 medium onion, finely chopped
1 large garlic clove, finely chopped	1 large garlic clove, finely chopped
225 g/8 oz button mushrooms, finely chopped	2 cups button mushrooms, finely chopped
50 g/2 oz butter	¼ cup butter
100 g/4 oz Ricotta cheese	½ cup Ricotta cheese
2 tablespoons plain yogurt	2 tablespoons plain yogurt
salt	salt
freshly ground black pepper	freshly ground black pepper
1 teaspoon grated nutmeg	½ teaspoon grated nutmeg
2 tablespoons Parmesan cheese	2 tablespoons Parmesan cheese

Using a sharp knife, scoop the flesh from the aubergine (eggplant) halves, leaving the skins intact. Chop the flesh quite finely, place on kitchen paper towels and sprinkle with salt. Sprinkle the inside of the aubergine (eggplant) skins with salt and place upside down on kitchen paper towels. Leave for 15 minutes, then pat dry with kitchen paper towels and squeeze out excess liquid. Place the skins and the chopped flesh in the grill (broiler) pan, sprinkle with the olive oil and grill (broil) for about 15 minutes, until soft but not brown.

Meanwhile, combine the onion, garlic and mushrooms and sauté gently in the butter. Add the softened chopped aubergine (eggplant) and cook together for another 5 minutes. Remove from the heat and add the remaining ingredients, except the Parmesan.

Spoon the mixture into the aubergine (eggplant) skins and place on a baking sheet. Sprinkle the top of each with Parmesan cheese. Bake in a preheated hot oven (220°C/425°F, Gas Mark 7) for 35 minutes, until nicely browned. Serve immediately.
Serves 8

Stuffed Tomatoes
(Photograph: Dutch Dairy Bureau)

Asparagus Vol-au-Vents

METRIC/IMPERIAL
225 g/8 oz frozen puff
   pastry, thawed, or
   eight 7.5 cm/3 inch,
   vol-au-vent cases
watercress to garnish
Filling:
450 g/1 lb asparagus,
   trimmed
50 g/2 oz butter
2 shallots, sliced
1 × 295 g/10½ oz can
   condensed asparagus
   soup
salt
freshly ground black
   pepper
1 tablespoon lemon juice

AMERICAN
½ lb frozen puff pastry,
   thawed, or eight 3 inch
   vol-au-vent cases
watercress to garnish
Filling:
1 lb asparagus, trimmed
¼ cup butter
2 shallots, sliced
1 × 10½ oz can
   condensed asparagus
   soup
salt
freshly ground black
   pepper
1 tablespoon lemon juice

If making your own vol-au-vent cases, roll out the
pastry and cut into sixteen 7.5 cm/3 inch rounds. Cut
the centres from 8 of the rounds, using a smaller cutter.
Place the 8 rounds on a baking sheet, brush with water
and place the 8 pastry rings on top. Bake in a preheated
hot oven (220°C/425°F, Gas Mark 7) for 30 minutes,
until well risen and golden brown.

Meanwhile, make the filling. Tie the asparagus in
bundles and stand them upright in a saucepan of
boiling salted water. Cover and cook for about 10
minutes, until just tender. The time will vary according
to the size of the asparagus. Take care not to overcook.
When just tender, drain and allow to cool.

Reserve 8 asparagus heads for garnish and chop the
remainder into 1 cm/½ inch pieces, discarding any
stringy stems. Melt the butter in a frying pan (skillet)
and gently sauté the shallots until soft but not brown.
Add the asparagus and the asparagus soup, salt,
pepper and lemon juice. Stir gently to mix, then spoon
into the vol-au-vent cases. Serve piping hot, garnished
with the reserved asparagus heads and watercress.

Both filling and cases can be made in advance and
put together at the last minute. Reheat for 10 minutes in
a preheated hot oven (220°C/425°F, Gas Mark 7) before
serving.
Serves 8

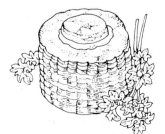

Crudités

METRIC/IMPERIAL
1 cauliflower
6 carrots
6 celery sticks
1 green pepper, cored
   and seeded
1 red pepper, cored and
   seeded
1 bunch radishes,
   trimmed
Avocado dip:
1 ripe avocado, stoned,
   peeled and sliced
100 g/4 oz Ricotta cheese
1 garlic clove, crushed
salt
freshly ground black
   pepper
Blue cheese dip:
100 g/4 oz crumbled
   Stilton cheese
100 g/4 oz cream cheese
2 tablespoons plain
   yogurt
salt
freshly ground black
   pepper
Herb dip:
250 ml/8 fl oz
   mayonnaise
1 garlic clove, crushed
1 tablespoon chopped
   fresh parsley
1 tablespoon chopped
   fresh basil
salt
freshly ground black
   pepper

AMERICAN
1 cauliflower
6 carrots
6 stalks celery
1 green pepper, cored
   and seeded
1 red pepper, cored and
   seeded
1 bunch radishes,
   trimmed
Avocado dip:
1 ripe avocado, pitted,
   peeled and sliced
½ cup Ricotta cheese
1 garlic clove, crushed
salt
freshly ground black
   pepper
Blue cheese dip:
½ cup crumbled Stilton
   cheese
½ cup cream cheese
2 tablespoons plain
   yogurt
salt
freshly ground black
   pepper
Herb dip:
1 cup mayonnaise
1 garlic clove, crushed
1 tablespoon chopped
   fresh parsley
1 tablespoon chopped
   fresh basil
salt
freshly ground black
   pepper

Break the cauliflower into florets and cut the carrots,
celery and peppers into julienne (matchstick) strips of
similar size.

Make up the dips by combining the ingredients for
each in a bowl or by processing briefly in a blender or
food processor.

To serve, arrange all the vegetables on a large platter
with the dip or dips in small bowls in the centre, or
serve on a special crudités dish.
Serves 12

Artichokes à la Café

METRIC/IMPERIAL	AMERICAN
4 globe artichokes	4 globe artichokes
120 ml/4 fl oz olive oil	½ cup olive oil
2 tablespoons vinegar	2 tablespoons vinegar

2 tablespoons strong
  black coffee
	2 tablespoons strong
	  black coffee

1 garlic clove, crushed	1 garlic clove, crushed
salt	salt

freshly ground black
  pepper
	freshly ground black
	  pepper

Cut the thick stems from the artichokes and trim the leaves with a pair of kitchen scissors. Place the artichokes in a large saucepan of boiling salted water, cover and simmer gently for 45 minutes. The artichokes are cooked when a leaf can be pulled out easily. Place the artichokes upside down in a colander and leave to drain.

Combine the oil, vinegar and coffee with the garlic, salt and pepper. Serve the artichokes cold with the coffee vinaigrette.
Serves 4

Julienne of Vegetables in Aspic

METRIC/IMPERIAL	AMERICAN

100 g/4 oz tiny haricots
  verts (French beans),
  trimmed
	1 cup tiny haricots verts
	  (green beans),
	  trimmed

6 carrots	6 carrots
2 celery sticks, trimmed	2 stalks celery, trimmed
3 small turnips, peeled	3 small turnips, peeled

2 tablespoons shelled
  fresh garden peas
	2 tablespoons shelled
	  fresh garden peas

600 ml/1 pint water	2½ cups water

aspic, sufficient to make
  600 ml/1 pint
	aspic, sufficient to make
	  2½ cups

2 tablespoons lemon
  juice
	2 tablespoons lemon
	  juice

To garnish:	**To garnish:**
lettuce hearts	lettuce hearts
mayonnaise	mayonnaise

Cook the beans in boiling salted water for about 5 minutes, until just tender. Drain and set aside. Cut the carrots, celery and turnips into julienne (matchstick) strips and cook separately in the same way, until just tender but not soft. Cook the carrots for about 10 minutes, the celery for about 15 minutes and the turnips for about 7 minutes. The cooking times may vary according to the size of the julienne strips. Cook the peas in the same way for about 3 minutes. Make up the aspic with 600 ml/1 pint (2½ cups) boiling water according to packet instructions. Allow to cool. Drain all the vegetables and allow to cool.

Arrange the vegetables carefully in the bottom of a bowl. Place the peas in the bottom and arrange the vegetable julienne strips in a wheel-shape on top. Add the lemon juice to the aspic mixture and pour very slowly over the vegetables, taking care not to disturb the vegetable pattern. Place the bowl in the refrigerator and allow to set.

Before serving, dip the bowl in hot water and invert the mould on to a serving platter. Shake gently to release. Garnish with lettuce hearts and mayonnaise.
Serves 6

Stuffed Courgettes (Zucchini)

METRIC/IMPERIAL	AMERICAN

6 large courgettes,
  trimmed
	6 large zucchini,
	  trimmed

2 tablespoons olive oil	2 tablespoons olive oil

2 medium onions,
  chopped
	2 medium onions,
	  chopped

2 garlic cloves, chopped	2 garlic cloves, chopped

6 medium mushrooms,
  chopped
	6 medium mushrooms,
	  chopped

1 × 227 g/8 oz can tomatoes	1 × 8 oz can tomatoes

2 tablespoons tomato
  purée
	2 tablespoons tomato
	  paste

1 tablespoon chopped
  fresh basil
	1 tablespoon chopped
	  fresh basil

2 tablespoons red wine	2 tablespoons red wine
salt	salt

freshly ground black
  pepper
	freshly ground black
	  pepper

grated Parmesan cheese
  to garnish
	grated Parmesan cheese
	  to garnish

Cut a thin slice lengthwise from each courgette (zucchini) and scoop out some of the flesh with a teaspoon. Chop the flesh and reserve. Place the courgettes (zucchini) in boiling salted water and boil for 5 minutes, then drain. Arrange the courgettes (zucchini) in an ovenproof dish and cover with foil.

Heat the oil in a saucepan and gently sauté the onions, garlic, mushrooms and courgette (zucchini) flesh until soft. Add the tomatoes and the tomato purée (paste). Cook together for 15 minutes, then add the basil, wine, salt and pepper. Cook for a further 5 minutes on a low heat, then spoon into the courgettes (zucchini). Just before serving, place in a preheated hot oven (220°C/425°F, Gas Mark 7) for 20 minutes. Serve sprinkled with Parmesan.
Serves 6

Note: This dish is also excellent served cold as an accompaniment to cold meats or cold chicken or, served as a light supper dish.

Stuffed Artichokes

Prepare and cook the artichokes as described on page 25. Remove the choke by cutting carefully with a sharp knife and scooping out with a spoon. Fill the artichokes with one of the following stuffings:

Vegetarian Stuffing

METRIC/IMPERIAL	AMERICAN
1 tablespoon olive oil	1 tablespoon olive oil
½ green pepper, cored, seeded and diced	½ green pepper, cored, seeded and diced
1 stick celery, chopped	1 stalk celery, chopped
1 tablespoon finely chopped onion	1 tablespoon finely chopped onion
50 g/2 oz mushrooms, chopped	½ cup mushrooms, chopped
½ vegetarian stock cube	1 vegetarian bouillon cube
150 ml/¼ pint tomato juice	⅔ cup tomato juice

Heat the oil and gently fry the pepper, celery, onion and mushroom. Add the tomato juice and crumble over the stock cube. Simmer for 30 minutes. Spoon into the artichokes. Serve hot or cold.
Makes stuffing for 2 artichokes

Yogurt and Herb Stuffing

METRIC/IMPERIAL	AMERICAN
150 g/5 oz plain yogurt	⅔ cup plain yogurt
1 tablespoon chopped chives	1 tablespoon chopped chives
1 teaspoon capers	1 teaspoon capers
½ teaspoon dried tarragon	½ teaspoon dried tarragon
50 g/2 oz peeled prawns	¼ cup shelled shrimp
2 unshelled prawns to garnish	2 unshelled shrimp to garnish

Combine all the ingredients and divide between the artichokes. Garnish with the unshelled prawns (shrimp).
Makes stuffing for 2 artichokes

Savoury Liver Stuffing

METRIC/IMPERIAL	AMERICAN
1 tablespoon olive oil	1 tablespoon olive oil
50 g/2 oz cooking apple, sliced	½ cup sliced cooking apple
100 g/4 oz chicken liver, chopped	½ cup chicken liver, chopped
150 ml/¼ pint chicken stock	⅔ cup chicken stock
1 tomato, chopped	1 tomato, chopped
2 tomato slices to garnish	2 tomato slices to garnish

Heat the oil and add the apple and chicken liver. Add the stock and tomato and simmer for 30 minutes. Stuff the artichokes and serve hot, garnished with a tomato slice.
Makes stuffing for 2 artichokes

Cauliflower Stuffing

METRIC/IMPERIAL	AMERICAN
175 g/6 oz cauliflower florets	1½ cups cauliflower florets
25 g/1 oz mushrooms, chopped	¼ cup mushrooms, chopped
2 tablespoons chopped ham	2 tablespoons chopped ham
50 g/2 oz cheddar cheese, grated	¼ cup grated cheddar cheese
1 tablespoon tomato ketchup	1 tablespoon tomato ketchup
1 tablespoon olive oil	1 tablespoon olive oil

Combine the cauliflower, mushrooms, ham and half the cheese. Mix in the tomato ketchup and oil and place in a casserole in a moderate oven (180°C/350°F, Gas Mark 4) for 45 minutes. Spoon into the artichokes and sprinkle over the remaining cheese. Place under a preheated grill until the cheese is melted and golden brown. Serve immediately.
Makes stuffing for 2 artichokes

Savoury Liver Stuffed Artichoke, Vegetarian Stuffing
Cauliflower Stuffed Artichoke, Artichoke with Yogurt and Herb Stuffing
(Photograph: Brittany Prince Artichokes)

Aubergine (Eggplant) Pâté

METRIC/IMPERIAL	AMERICAN
2 aubergines, trimmed	2 eggplants, trimmed
grated rind and juice of 1 lemon	grated rind and juice of 1 lemon
2 tablespoons tahini paste	2 tablespoons tahini paste
½ teaspoon grated nutmeg	½ teaspoon grated nutmeg
1 teaspoon salt	1 teaspoon salt
freshly ground black pepper	freshly ground black pepper
wholewheat toast to serve	wholewheat toast to serve

Place the aubergines (eggplants) under a hot grill (broiler) and grill (broil) for about 20 minutes, turning frequently, until quite burnt on all sides. Allow the aubergines (eggplants) to cool, then halve them lengthwise and scrape the flesh out into a bowl. Discard the shells. Add the lemon rind and juice, tahini, nutmeg, salt and pepper to taste and combine thoroughly. Alternatively, this can be done in a food processor or blender. Serve with fingers of wholewheat toast.
Serves 6

Asparagus Mousse

METRIC/IMPERIAL	AMERICAN
12 large asparagus stalks, trimmed	12 large asparagus stalks, trimmed
50 g/2 oz butter	¼ cup butter
1 medium onion, chopped	1 medium onion, chopped
1 garlic clove, chopped	1 garlic clove, chopped
300 ml/½ pint chicken stock or water	1¼ cups chicken stock or water
salt	salt
freshly ground black pepper	freshly ground black pepper
1 × 295 g/10½ oz can condensed asparagus soup	1 × 10½ oz can condensed asparagus soup
3 teaspoons (1 envelope) powdered gelatine	1 envelope unflavored gelatin
120 ml/4 fl oz hot water	½ cup hot water
To garnish:	**To garnish:**
2 hard-boiled eggs, chopped	2 hard-cooked eggs, chopped
1 bunch watercress	1 bunch watercress

Tie the asparagus stalks in two bundles. Stand them upright in a saucepan of boiling salted water and cook for about 10 minutes, until just tender. Drain well and remove the ties. Reserve two asparagus stalks to garnish and chop the remainder into 1 cm/½ inch pieces, discarding any stringy ends.

Melt the butter in a frying pan (skillet) over a low heat and sauté the onion and garlic until tender but not brown. Add the asparagus, stock or water, salt and pepper and simmer gently for about 10 minutes. Allow to cool slightly, then transfer to a food processor or blender and process for about 1 minute. Add the asparagus soup and process again for another minute. Alternatively, press through a sieve.

Sprinkle the gelatine on to the hot water and stir to dissolve thoroughly. Add to the asparagus mixture and stir well, or process again briefly. Pour into a 900 ml/1½ pint (3¾ cup) mould and leave in the refrigerator to set.

Before serving, dip the mould in hot water, then invert the mousse on to a serving platter. Garnish with chopped egg, the reserved asparagus and watercress.
Serves 8

Cucumber Mousse

METRIC/IMPERIAL	AMERICAN
1 medium cucumber, peeled and sliced	1 medium cucumber, peeled and sliced
6 medium spring onions, trimmed and sliced	6 medium scallions, trimmed and sliced
1 medium potato, cooked and chopped	1 medium potato, cooked and chopped
2 garlic cloves, crushed	2 garlic cloves, crushed
1 teaspoon salt	1 teaspoon salt
225 g/8 oz cream cheese	1 cup cream cheese
freshly ground black pepper	freshly ground black pepper
3 teaspoons (1 envelope) powdered gelatine	1 envelope unflavored gelatin
2 tablespoons hot water	2 tablespoons hot water
2 tablespoons lemon juice	2 tablespoons lemon juice
slices of lemon to garnish	slices of lemon to garnish
To serve:	**To serve:**
brown bread and butter	brown bread and butter

Place the cucumber, spring onions (scallions), potato and garlic in a food processor or blender and process for 1 minute. Add the salt, cream cheese and pepper and process again briefly.

Sprinkle the gelatine over the lemon juice in a small heatproof bowl and leave to soften. Add the hot water. To ensure that it has thoroughly dissolved, stand the bowl in a saucepan of simmering water. Allow to cool, then add to the cucumber mixture. Process briefly and pour into a mould. Set in the refrigerator.

Before serving, dip the mould in hot water, then invert the mousse on to a serving platter. Garnish with lemon slices and serve with brown bread and butter. The mousse may also be set and served in individual ramekin dishes.
Serves 8

Leek and Tomato Tartlets

METRIC/IMPERIAL	AMERICAN
225 g/8 oz frozen shortcrust pastry, thawed	½ lb frozen basic pie dough, thawed
50 g/2 oz butter	¼ cup butter
2 medium leeks, sliced and thoroughly washed	2 medium leeks, sliced and thoroughly washed
2 large tomatoes, sliced	2 large tomatoes, sliced
4 large eggs, beaten	4 large eggs, beaten
120 ml/4 fl oz plain yogurt	½ cup plain yogurt
50 g/2 oz grated Cheddar cheese	½ cup grated Cheddar cheese
salt	salt
freshly ground black pepper	freshly ground black pepper
2 tablespoons chopped fresh chives	2 tablespoons chopped fresh chives

Roll out the pastry (dough) and cut into eight 8.5 cm/3½ inch diameter circles. Use to line eight individual flan tins (pie pans).

Melt the butter in a frying pan (skillet) and gently sauté the leeks until just tender. Divide between the eight pastry cases (pie shells) and place a slice of tomato in each. Combine the eggs, yogurt, cheese, salt and pepper. Divide between the eight tartlets and sprinkle with chopped chives. Place the tartlets on a baking sheet and bake in a preheated moderately hot oven (200°C/400°F, Gas Mark 6) for 35 minutes.
Serves 8

Hummus

METRIC/IMPERIAL	AMERICAN
225 g/½ lb dried chick peas or 1 × 400 g/14 oz can chick peas	1 cup dried chick peas or 1 × 14 oz can chick peas
100 g/4 oz tahini paste	½ cup tahini paste
3 tablespoons olive oil	3 tablespoons olive oil
3 garlic cloves, crushed	3 garlic cloves, crushed
grated rind and juice of 1 large lemon	grated rind and juice of 1 large lemon
1 teaspoon salt	1 teaspoon salt
freshly ground black pepper	freshly ground black pepper
To garnish:	**To garnish:**
6 olives	6 olives
1 tablespoon olive oil	1 tablespoon olive oil
To serve:	**To serve:**
wholewheat pitta bread, warmed	wholewheat pitta bread, warmed

If using dried chick peas, which have a very special, individual flavour, soak them overnight in plenty of cold water. Next day, drain the chick peas and simmer gently in fresh salted water for 1½ hours, until tender, then drain. If using canned chick peas for speed and convenience, simply drain them in a sieve.

Combine all the ingredients in a food processor or blender and process for 1 minute. Taste and correct the seasoning if necessary, then process again briefly. Spoon into a serving bowl or on to individual plates and garnish with olives and a little olive oil. Serve with warm wholewheat pitta bread.
Serves 12

Okra Provençal

METRIC/IMPERIAL	AMERICAN
4 tablespoons olive oil	¼ cup olive oil
2 medium onions, chopped	2 medium onions, chopped
2 garlic cloves, crushed	2 garlic cloves, crushed
1 × 400 g/14 oz can tomatoes	1 × 14 oz can tomatoes
2 tablespoons tomato purée	2 tablespoons tomato paste
1 teaspoon dried basil	1 teaspoon dried basil
2 bay leaves	2 bay leaves
1 teaspoon paprika	1 teaspoon paprika
2 tablespoons lemon juice	2 tablespoons lemon juice
salt	salt
freshly ground black pepper	freshly ground black pepper
450 g/1 lb small okra	1 lb small okra
2 tablespoons chopped fresh parsley to garnish	2 tablespoons chopped fresh parsley to garnish

Heat the oil in a frying pan (skillet) and sauté the onions and garlic until just translucent. Add the tomatoes, tomato purée (paste), basil, bay leaves, paprika, lemon juice, salt and pepper. Cook together over a low heat for about 15 minutes.

Meanwhile, trim the okra, being careful to cut off just the tail and not the whole end to prevent the juices escaping during cooking. Add the okra to the pan and continue cooking for another 15 minutes or until the okra are tender. Remove the bay leaves and serve garnished with chopped parsley.
Serves 8

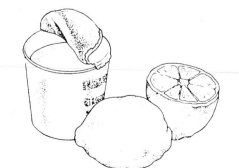

MAIN COURSES

The vegetables used in the following recipes can be varied according to their availability. Many of the dishes are perfect for vegetarians, and they can be served with cheese and nuts for added protein. A little meat, poultry or fish can be successfully added to most of these dishes.

Carrot and Almond Loaf with Tomato Sauce

METRIC/IMPERIAL	AMERICAN
50 g/2 oz butter	¼ cup butter
1 medium onion, sliced	1 medium onion, sliced
2 garlic cloves, chopped	2 garlic cloves, chopped
275 g/10 oz fresh wholewheat breadcrumbs	3 cups soft wholewheat bread crumbs
225 g/8 oz carrots, grated	2½ cups grated carrot
100 g/4 oz flaked almonds, toasted	1 cup slivered almonds, toasted
2 eggs, beaten	2 eggs, beaten
juice of 1 lemon	juice of 1 lemon
1 tablespoon chopped fresh parsley	1 tablespoon chopped fresh parsley
1 teaspoon grated nutmeg	1 teaspoon grated nutmeg
salt	salt
freshly ground black pepper	freshly ground black pepper
Tomato sauce:	**Tomato sauce:**
2 tablespoons olive oil	2 tablespoons olive oil
1 medium onion, sliced	1 medium onion, sliced
1 garlic clove, chopped	1 garlic clove, chopped
1 × 400 g/14 oz can tomatoes	1 × 14 oz can tomatoes
2 tablespoons tomato purée	2 tablespoons tomato paste
1 tablespoon chopped fresh basil	1 tablespoon chopped fresh basil
salt	salt
freshly ground black pepper	freshly ground black pepper

Melt the butter in a heavy frying pan (skillet) over a low heat and gently sauté the onion and garlic for 5 minutes until just translucent but not brown. Meanwhile, in a large bowl, combine the breadcrumbs, carrot and almonds. Add the onion and garlic and stir well. Add the beaten eggs, lemon juice, parsley, nutmeg and salt and pepper and combine well. Add a little water if more liquid is required, then spoon the mixture into a greased 19 × 13 × 8.5 cm/7½ × 5 × 3½ inch loaf tin (pan) and bake in a preheated moderately hot oven (200°C/400°F, Gas Mark 6) for 45 minutes or until nicely browned and a sharp knife inserted in the centre comes out clean.

Towards the end of the cooking time, prepare the tomato sauce. Heat the oil in a frying pan (skillet) and sauté the onion and garlic for about 5 minutes, until just translucent. Add the tomatoes, tomato purée (paste), basil, salt and pepper, stir well and simmer gently until the carrot loaf is cooked. Serve immediately.
Serves 8

Carrot and Almond Loaf with Tomato Sauce

Vegetable Curry

METRIC/IMPERIAL	AMERICAN
50 g/2 oz butter	¼ cup butter
2 tablespoons olive oil	2 tablespoons olive oil
6 whole cloves	6 whole cloves
6 whole cardamoms	6 whole cardamoms
4 medium onions, sliced	4 medium onions, sliced
2 garlic cloves, chopped	2 garlic cloves, chopped
2 celery sticks, sliced	2 stalks celery, sliced
2 carrots, sliced	2 carrots, sliced
3 courgettes, sliced	3 zucchini, sliced
1 parsnip, peeled and chopped	1 parsnip, peeled and chopped
2 potatoes, chopped	2 potatoes, chopped
3 broccoli spears, broken into florets	3 broccoli spears, broken into florets
100 g/4 oz shelled fresh or frozen peas	¾ cup shelled fresh or frozen peas
1 × 400 g/14 oz can tomatoes	1 × 14 oz can tomatoes
1 teaspoon grated nutmeg	1 teaspoon grated nutmeg
1 teaspoon ground coriander	1 teaspoon ground coriander
1 teaspoon salt	1 teaspoon salt
1 teaspoon paprika	1 teaspoon paprika
1 tablespoon curry powder	1 tablespoon curry powder
2 bay leaves	2 bay leaves
1 kg/2 lb brown rice, soaked and drained	2 lb brown rice, soaked and drained
1 tablespoon chopped fresh parsley to garnish	1 tablespoon chopped fresh parsley to garnish

Heat the butter and oil in a large frying pan (skillet) over a low heat. Add the cloves and cardamom seeds and stir until they pop. Add the onions, garlic and celery and cook for about 10 minutes, then add the carrots, courgettes (zucchini) and parsnip. Cook together briefly, then add the potatoes and broccoli florets. Continue cooking for 10 minutes, then add the peas and the can of tomatoes, plus a can of water. Add the nutmeg, coriander, salt, paprika, curry powder and bay leaves and continue cooking over a low heat for 35 minutes, until all the vegetables are tender.

Cook the brown rice in a large saucepan in twice as much boiling salted water for about 45 minutes, until all the water has been absorbed and the rice is tender. Serve the curry on a bed of brown rice, sprinkled with chopped parsley.
Serves 8

Stuffed Vine Leaves

METRIC/IMPERIAL	AMERICAN
1 × 225 g/8 oz packet vine leaves	1 × ½ lb packet vine leaves
225 g/8 oz long-grain rice	1 cup long-grain rice
2 medium onions, finely chopped	2 medium onions, finely chopped
2 garlic cloves, finely chopped	2 garlic cloves, finely chopped
1 red pepper, cored, seeded and finely chopped	1 red pepper, cored, seeded and finely chopped
1 courgette, finely chopped	1 zucchini, finely chopped
1 tablespoon chopped fresh basil	1 tablespoon chopped fresh basil
2 tablespoons flaked almonds, toasted	2 tablespoons slivered almonds, toasted
1 teaspoon mixed spice	1 teaspoon ground allspice
1 teaspoon grated nutmeg	1 teaspoon grated nutmeg
juice of 1 lemon	juice of 1 lemon
120 ml/4 fl oz vegetable oil	½ cup vegetable oil
300 ml/½ pint water	1¼ cups water
1 teaspoon salt	1 teaspoon salt

Soak the vine leaves in boiling water for 30 minutes. Drain, pick out any broken leaves and reserve them. Place the rice in a large mixing bowl and add the onions, garlic, red pepper and courgette (zucchini), making sure everything is very finely chopped. Add the basil, almonds, spice and nutmeg and mix thoroughly.

To stuff the vine leaves, spread each leaf, vein-side-up on a board and place 1 teaspoon of the rice and vegetable mixture in the centre. Make a parcel by folding and rolling up the leaf. Continue until all the vine leaves and stuffing have been used.

Use the reserved broken vine leaves to line a large heavy saucepan. (If you do not have enough broken vine leaves, use lettuce or spinach.) Pack the stuffed vine leaves quite tightly in layers in the saucepan. Beat together the lemon juice, oil, water and salt and pour this over the vine leaves. Cover tightly with a lid and simmer gently for 2 hours. Add more water if necessary and take care the stuffed vine leaves do not burn. Serve hot or cold.
Serves 8

Spring Vegetable Vol-au-Vent

METRIC/IMPERIAL	AMERICAN
1 × 225 g/8 oz packet frozen puff pastry, thawed	1 × 8 oz packet frozen puff pastry, thawed
Filling:	**Filling:**
50 g/2 oz butter	¼ cup butter
3 leeks, sliced and thoroughly washed	3 leeks, sliced and thoroughly washed
2 medium carrots, sliced	2 medium carrots, sliced
1 small red pepper, cored, seeded and chopped	1 small red pepper, cored, seeded and chopped
100 g/4 oz button mushrooms	1 cup button mushrooms
1 × 350 g/12 oz can sweetcorn, drained	1 × 12 oz can whole kernel corn, drained
Hollandaise sauce:	**Hollandaise sauce:**
225 g/8 oz unsalted butter	1 cup unsalted butter
3 egg yolks	3 egg yolks
1 tablespoon lemon juice	1 tablespoon lemon juice
salt	salt
freshly ground pepper	freshly ground pepper

Roll out the pastry about 5 mm/¼ inch thick and cut into two pieces of the same size and shape – round, oval or square. Place one piece of pastry on top of the other and cut out the centre of the top piece leaving a 2.5 cm/1 inch border. Dampen with water between the border and base and press together firmly. Reserve the piece cut from the centre to use as a lid for the vol-au-vent. Place the pastry case and lid on a dampened baking sheet and bake in a preheated hot oven (220°C/425°F, Gas Mark 7) for about 35 minutes, until well risen and golden brown.

To make the filling, melt the butter in a heavy frying pan (skillet) over a low heat and gently sauté the leeks and peppers for 5 to 10 minutes until soft. Cook the carrots in boiling salted water for about 15 minutes, until just tender. Blanch the mushrooms in boiling salted water for 2 minutes. Drain the carrots, red pepper and mushrooms and add to the leeks in the frying pan (skillet) with the sweetcorn. Cover and keep warm but do not allow to cook any further as the vegetables should retain some crispness.

To make the Hollandaise sauce, reserve a knob of the butter and gently heat the remainder in a small saucepan until melted but not separated. Place the egg yolks in the top of a double boiler or in a heatproof bowl and beat well. Place in position over gently simmering water. Have a bowl of cold water by you so that you can quickly reduce the heat if the sauce begins to curdle. As the eggs heat, gradually begin to add the melted butter, stirring all the time, adding it more quickly as the eggs begin to incorporate the butter. If the sauce shows any sign of 'scrambling', quickly transfer the top of the double boiler or the bowl to the cold water for a moment and add 1 tablespoon cold water. When all the butter is incorporated, add the lemon juice, salt and pepper. Beat well and finally beat in the reserved knob of butter.

Place the warm vegetables in the vol-au-vent case and cover with hot sauce. Place the pastry lid in position and serve immediately.
Serves 8

Vegetable Strudel

METRIC/IMPERIAL	AMERICAN
½ packet filo pastry (see Note)	½ packet filo pastry (see Note)
175 g/6 oz butter, melted	¾ cup butter, melted
225 g/8 oz flat mushrooms, sliced	½ lb flat mushrooms, sliced
2 medium onions, sliced	2 medium onions, sliced
2 garlic cloves, chopped	2 garlic cloves, chopped
1 × 400 g/14 oz can tomatoes	1 × 14 oz can tomatoes
3 courgettes, sliced	3 zucchini, sliced
salt	salt
freshly ground black pepper	freshly ground black pepper

Lay out the sheets of filo pastry and cover with plastic wrap or a clean damp cloth. Put 2 tablespoons melted butter in a frying pan (skillet) and sauté the mushrooms, onions and garlic for 10 minutes. Season with salt and pepper, transfer to a bowl and leave on one side. In the same frying pan (skillet), combine the tomatoes and courgettes (zucchini). Cook together gently for about 10 minutes, then season with salt and pepper and allow to cool.

Brush the inside of a 33 × 23 cm/13 × 9 inch roasting tin (pan) with melted butter and fit one sheet of filo pastry in the bottom, allowing it to come slightly up the sides. Brush with melted butter and cover with a thin layer of the mushroom mixture. Continue layering, alternating mushroom and courgette (zucchini) mixture, and interleaving each layer with a sheet of filo pastry brushed with melted butter. End with a layer of filo pastry. Brush generously with melted butter and bake in a preheated moderately hot oven (200°C/400°F, Gas Mark 6) for 20 minutes until golden brown on top.
Serves 8

Note: Filo pastry is available from delicatessens and Greek food shops (see page 19). This recipe is ideal for using up any leftover vegetables and is excellent with spinach and cheese. Meat may also be added, if liked.

Three Bean Casserole

METRIC/IMPERIAL	AMERICAN
175 g/6 oz dried butter beans, soaked overnight and drained or 1 × 400 g/14 oz can butter beans, drained	1 cup dried butter beans, soaked overnight and drained or 1 × 14 oz can butter beans, drained
175 g/6 oz dried red kidney beans, soaked overnight and drained or 1 × 400 g/14 oz can red kidney beans, drained	1 cup dried red kidney beans, soaked overnight and drained or 1 × 14 oz can red kidney beans, drained
175 g/6 oz dried black-eye beans, soaked overnight and drained or 1 × 400 g/14 oz can black-eye beans, drained	1 cup dried black-eye beans, soaked overnight and drained or 1 × 14 oz can black-eye beans, drained
50 g/2 oz butter	¼ cup butter
2 medium onions, sliced	2 medium onions, sliced
2 garlic cloves, chopped	2 garlic cloves, chopped
1 × 400 g/14 oz can tomatoes	1 × 14 oz can tomatoes
2 celery sticks, sliced	2 stalks celery, sliced
2 courgettes, sliced	2 zucchini, sliced
1 bay leaf	1 bay leaf
2.5 cm/1 inch ginger root, grated	1 inch ginger root, grated
1 teaspoon grated nutmeg	1 teaspoon grated nutmeg
1 teaspoon ground cumin	1 teaspoon ground cumin
1 teaspoon ground coriander	1 teaspoon ground coriander
salt	salt
freshly ground black pepper	freshly ground black pepper

If using dried beans, this dish is ideal for cooking in a pressure cooker. If using canned beans, cook in a casserole in the oven.

Melt the butter in a large frying pan (skillet) over a low heat and gently sauté the onions and garlic for about 5 minutes, until soft. Add the can of tomatoes and their juice, plus 2 cans of water and bring to the boil. Simmer for about 5 minutes, then add the remaining ingredients. Cook for a further 5 minutes.

Place the beans in a casserole or pressure cooker and add the vegetable mixture. Stir well, taste and correct the seasoning if necessary. Cook in the casserole in a preheated moderately hot oven (190°C/375°F, Gas Mark 5) for 1 hour. If using a pressure cooker, bring to high pressure and cook for 20 minutes. Remove the pressure cooker from the heat and allow the pressure to reduce at room temperature.
Serves 8

Cauliflower and Fennel au Gratin

METRIC/IMPERIAL	AMERICAN
1 cauliflower, washed and outer leaves removed	1 cauliflower, washed and outer leaves removed
1 bulb fennel, trimmed	1 bulb fennel, trimmed
50 g/2 oz butter	¼ cup butter
50 g/2 oz plain flour	½ cup all-purpose flour
600 ml/1 pint milk	2½ cups milk
50 g/2 oz Stilton cheese, crumbled	½ cup crumbled Stilton cheese
salt	salt
freshly ground black pepper	freshly ground black pepper
5 tablespoons fresh white breadcrumbs	5 tablespoons soft white bread crumbs
3 tablespoons melted butter	3 tablespoons melted butter

Cut the cauliflower and fennel into quarters and cook in boiling salted water for 15 minutes, until just tender but still firm. Drain well.

Meanwhile, melt the butter in a saucepan, add the flour and cook, stirring, for 1 minute. Remove from the heat and gradually add the milk, then bring to the boil, stirring continuously. Add the cheese, salt and pepper and cook for a further minute.

Place the cauliflower and fennel in an ovenproof dish and pour over the cheese sauce. Combine the breadcrumbs with the melted butter and sprinkle over the top. Bake in a preheated hot oven (220°C/425°F, Gas Mark 7) for 25 minutes. Serve immediately.
Serves 4

Three Bean Casserole
Cauliflower and Fennel au Gratin

Winter Vegetable Pie

METRIC/IMPERIAL	AMERICAN
Pastry:	**Dough:**
225 g/8 oz plain flour	2 cups all-purpose flour
pinch of salt	pinch of salt
50 g/2 oz butter	¼ cup butter
50 g/2 oz lard	¼ cup shortening
about 120 ml/4 fl oz iced water	about ½ cup iced water
Filling:	**Filling:**
225 g/8 oz red lentils, rinsed	1 cup red lentils, rinsed
2 tablespoons olive oil	2 tablespoons olive oil
2 potatoes, peeled and diced	2 potatoes, peeled and diced
2 parsnips, peeled and diced	2 parsnips, peeled and diced
2 carrots, sliced	2 carrots, sliced
2 medium onions, sliced	2 medium onions, sliced
100 g/4 oz shelled fresh or frozen peas	¾ cup shelled fresh or frozen peas
1 × 400 g/14 oz can tomatoes	1 × 14 oz can tomatoes
2 bay leaves	2 bay leaves
1 teaspoon salt	1 teaspoon salt
1 teaspoon cumin powder	1 teaspoon cumin powder
1 teaspoon grated nutmeg	1 teaspoon grated nutmeg
1 teaspoon mixed dried herbs	1 teaspoon mixed dried herbs
1 egg, beaten	1 egg, beaten

To make the pastry (dough), sift the flour and salt into a bowl and rub (cut) in the butter and lard (shortening) until the mixture resembles fine breadcrumbs. Add sufficient water to make a soft dough, cover with plastic wrap and leave in the refrigerator while making the filling.

Heat the oil in a heavy saucepan and sauté the potatoes, parsnips, carrots and onions for 5 minutes, until soft. Add the peas, cover and cook over a low heat for 10 minutes, stirring occasionally. Add the lentils to the pan with the tomatoes, bay leaves, salt, cumin, nutmeg and mixed herbs. Mix well, cover and cook for a further 10 minutes until the vegetables are soft. Transfer to a 20 × 25 cm/8 × 10 inch ovenproof pie dish and allow to cool.

Place a pie funnel in the centre of the dish and dampen the rim with a little water. Roll out the pastry (dough) 5 cm/2 inches wider than the dish and cut a 2.5 cm/1 inch strip from the outer edge. Use to line the rim of the pie dish and dampen with a little water. Cover with the pastry (dough) lid, sealing the edges well. Trim and flute the edges and decorate with leaves cut from the pastry (dough) trimmings. Cut a small hole in the centre to allow steam to escape. Brush with beaten egg and bake in a preheated moderately hot oven (190°C/375°F, Gas Mark 5) for 45 minutes, until golden.
Serves 8

Variation: Add other spices, such as curry powder, and a little chopped gammon or beef.

Mushroom Timbale

METRIC/IMPERIAL	AMERICAN
50 g/2 oz butter	¼ cup butter
450 g/1 lb flat mushrooms, chopped	1 lb flat mushrooms, chopped
1 onion, sliced	1 onion, sliced
1 garlic clove, chopped	1 garlic clove, chopped
2 eggs, beaten	2 eggs, beaten
2 egg yolks	2 egg yolks
2 tablespoons black coffee	2 tablespoons black coffee
150 ml/¼ pint single cream	⅔ cup light cream
salt	salt
freshly ground black pepper	freshly ground black pepper
White sauce:	**White sauce:**
50 g/2 oz butter	¼ cup butter
50 g/2 oz plain flour	½ cup all-purpose flour
300 ml/½ pint milk	1¼ cups milk
salt	salt
freshly ground pepper	freshly ground pepper
To garnish:	**To garnish:**
4 slices fried bread, halved diagonally	4 slices fried bread, halved diagonally
1 bunch watercress	1 bunch watercress

Melt the butter in a heavy frying pan (skillet) over a low heat. Add the mushrooms, onion and garlic and cook gently together for about 15 minutes. Meanwhile, make the white sauce by melting the butter in a small saucepan. Add the flour and cook together for 1 minute, stirring. Remove from the heat and gradually add the milk, stirring continuously. Bring to the boil, stirring, then remove from the heat and allow to cool, stirring occasionally.

Place the mushroom mixture, the eggs, egg yolks, coffee, cream, salt and pepper in a food processor or blender and process for 1 minute. Add the white sauce and process again briefly.

Butter a 900 ml/1½ pint (3¾ cup) ring mould and pour in the timbale mixture. Stand the mould in a bain marie of hot water and bake in a preheated moderate oven (180°C/350°F, Gas Mark 4) for 25 minutes or until a knife inserted in the mixture comes out clean. Invert the timbale carefully on to a serving platter and garnish with triangles of fried bread and watercress.
Serves 6

Aubergine (Eggplant) and Potato Moussaka

METRIC/IMPERIAL	AMERICAN
3 medium aubergines, thinly sliced	3 medium eggplants, thinly sliced
sea salt	sea salt
3 medium potatoes	3 medium potatoes
50 g/2 oz butter	¼ cup butter
2 onions, sliced	2 onions, sliced
2 garlic cloves, chopped	2 garlic cloves, chopped
1 × 400 g/14 oz can tomatoes	1 × 14 oz can tomatoes
2 tablespoons tomato purée	2 tablespoons tomato paste
2 bay leaves	2 bay leaves
1 teaspoon grated nutmeg	1 teaspoon grated nutmeg
1 teaspoon dried basil	1 teaspoon dried basil
1 teaspoon oregano	1 teaspoon oregano
100 g/4 oz cottage cheese	½ cup cottage cheese
120 ml/4 fl oz plain yogurt	½ cup plain yogurt
2 eggs, beaten	2 eggs, beaten
150 ml/¼ pint milk	⅔ cup milk
freshly ground black pepper	freshly ground black pepper
4 tablespoons grated Parmesan cheese	4 tablespoons grated Parmesan cheese

Lay out the slices of aubergine (eggplant) on kitchen paper towels and sprinkle with salt. Leave for 15 minutes, then pat dry with paper towels, turn the slices over and repeat for the other sides. Peel the potatoes and cook in boiling salted water for about 10 minutes, until almost cooked. Drain, allow to cool and slice thinly.

Melt the butter in a heavy frying pan (skillet) over a low heat and gently sauté the onions and garlic. Cook for about 10 minutes, then add the tomatoes, plus a can of water, the tomato purée (paste), bay leaves, nutmeg, 1 teaspoon sea salt, basil and oregano. Bring to the boil, then reduce the heat slightly and cook for 30 minutes, until the tomato sauce has thickened. Remove the bay leaves.

Put a little of the tomato sauce in the bottom of a 20 × 25 cm/8 × 10 inch ovenproof dish and cover with a layer of aubergine (eggplant), then a layer of potato, then a little cottage cheese. Repeat the layers until all the ingredients have been used up. Beat together the yogurt, eggs, milk and a little salt and pepper and pour over the moussaka. Sprinkle with Parmesan cheese and bake in a preheated moderately hot oven (200°C/400°F, Gas Mark 6) for 1 hour, until nicely browned and bubbling. Serve immediately with a green salad.
Serves 8

Leek, Courgette (Zucchini) and Tomato Quiche

METRIC/IMPERIAL	AMERICAN
Pastry:	**Dough:**
225 g/8 oz plain flour	2 cups all-purpose flour
pinch of salt	pinch of salt
50 g/2 oz butter	¼ cup butter
50 g/2 oz lard	¼ cup shortening
about 120 ml/4 fl oz iced water	about ½ cup iced water
Filling:	**Filling:**
50 g/2 oz butter	¼ cup butter
3 leeks, sliced and thoroughly washed	3 leeks, sliced and thoroughly washed
1 courgette, sliced	1 zucchini, sliced
1 garlic clove, chopped	1 garlic clove, chopped
4 large eggs, beaten	4 large eggs, beaten
4 tablespoons plain yogurt	4 tablespoons plain yogurt
120 ml/4 fl oz milk	½ cup milk
100 g/4 oz mature Cheddar cheese, grated	1 cup shredded sharp Cheddar cheese
salt	salt
freshly ground black pepper	freshly ground black pepper
1 large tomato, sliced	1 large tomato, sliced
2 tablespoons chopped fresh parsley to garnish	2 tablespoons chopped fresh parsley to garnish

To make the pastry (dough), sift the flour and salt together into a bowl and rub (cut) in the butter and lard (shortening) until the mixture resembles fine bread-crumbs. Add sufficient iced water to mix to a soft dough, form into a ball, wrap in plastic wrap and leave in the refrigerator to rest.

Meanwhile, make the filling. Melt the butter in a heavy frying pan (skillet) and gently sauté the leeks, courgette (zucchini) and garlic for about 7 minutes, until quite tender. Remove from the heat. Place the eggs, yogurt, milk, cheese, salt and pepper in a bowl and beat well to combine.

Roll out the pastry quite thinly and use to line a 20 cm/8 inch flan tin (quiche pan) or dish, fluting the edge if necessary. Fill the quiche with the leek mixture and pour over the egg mixture. Even the surface, then arrange the tomato slices on top. Bake in a preheated moderately hot oven (190°C/375°F, Gas Mark 5) for 45 minutes or until set and golden brown. Garnish with parsley.
Serves 4 to 6

Vegetable Lasagne

METRIC/IMPERIAL	AMERICAN
100 g/4 oz green lasagne	¼ lb green lasagne
1 teaspoon olive oil	noodles
450 g/1 lb spinach, stalks	1 teaspoon olive oil
removed, or 8 oz	1 lb spinach, stalks
chopped frozen	removed, or ½ lb
spinach	chopped, frozen
225 g/8 oz cottage cheese	spinach
100 g/4 oz chopped	1 cup cottage cheese
walnuts	1 cup chopped walnuts
2 tablespoons grated	2 tablespoons grated
Parmesan cheese	Parmesan cheese
Tomato sauce:	**Tomato sauce:**
2 tablespoons olive oil	2 tablespoons olive oil
2 medium onions,	2 medium onions,
chopped	chopped
1 garlic clove, chopped	1 garlic clove, chopped
1 × 400 g/14 oz can	1 × 14 oz can tomatoes
tomatoes	2 tablespoons tomato
2 tablespoons tomato	paste
purée	salt
salt	freshly ground black
freshly ground black	pepper
pepper	**Cheese sauce:**
Cheese sauce:	¼ cup butter
50 g/2 oz butter	½ cup all-purpose flour
50 g/2 oz plain flour	2½ cups milk
600 ml/1 pint milk	½ cup shredded
100 g/4 oz grated	Cheddar cheese
Cheddar cheese	salt
salt	freshly ground pepper
freshly ground pepper	

Place the lasagne in a large saucepan of boiling salted water with 1 teaspoon olive oil added to separate the pasta and cook for about 12 minutes. Drain and drape the pasta pieces around a mixing bowl to prevent them sticking together.

Cook the spinach in a very little boiling salted water for about 5 minutes, until tender. Drain and finely chop. If using frozen spinach, cook according to the instructions on the packet. Combine the spinach, cottage cheese and walnuts to make a thick paste.

To make the tomato sauce, heat the oil in a frying pan (skillet) and sauté the onion and garlic for about 5 minutes, until just translucent. Add the tomatoes, tomato purée (paste) and season to taste with salt and pepper.

To make the cheese sauce, melt the butter in a saucepan, add the flour and cook for 1 minute. Remove from the heat and gradually add the milk. Bring to the boil, stirring, until thickened, then add the cheese and salt and pepper to taste.

Grease a shallow oblong or square ovenproof dish and line with half the lasagne. Layer the tomato sauce, cheese sauce, spinach mixture and remaining lasagne, ending with a layer of cheese sauce. Sprinkle the top with Parmesan cheese and bake in a preheated moderately hot oven (200°C/400°F, Gas Mark 6) for 30 minutes. Serve immediately with a green salad.
Serves 4 to 6

Fettuccine with Courgettes (Zucchini) and Mushrooms

METRIC/IMPERIAL	AMERICAN
50 g/2 oz butter	¼ cup butter
1 medium onion, sliced	1 medium onion, sliced
1 garlic clove, chopped	1 garlic clove, chopped
450 g/1 lb courgettes,	1 lb zucchini, grated
grated	2 cups button
225 g/8 oz button	mushrooms, sliced
mushrooms, sliced	1¼ cups light cream
300 ml/½ pint single	1 lb fettuccine
cream	½ teaspoon grated
450 g/1 lb fettuccine	nutmeg
½ teaspoon grated	½ teaspoon salt
nutmeg	freshly ground black
½ teaspoon salt	pepper
freshly ground black	1 tablespoon chopped
pepper	fresh parsley to garnish
1 tablespoon chopped	
fresh parsley to garnish	

Melt the butter in a heavy frying pan (skillet) over a low heat. Add the onion and garlic and sauté until just translucent. Add the courgettes (zucchini) and the mushrooms, mixing well together. Cook gently, stirring occasionally, for about 10 minutes.

Meanwhile, bring some salted water to the boil in a large saucepan, and add the fettuccine. Boil for about 7 minutes, until just 'al dente', then drain.

Add the cream to the courgette and mushroom mixture with the nutmeg, salt and pepper. Combine with the fettuccine and serve immediately, garnished with chopped parsley.
Serves 6

Spinach Lasagne
Fettuccine with Courgette and Mushroom

Spinach, Parsnip and Carrot Layer

METRIC/IMPERIAL	AMERICAN
1 kg/2 lb spinach, trimmed and washed	2 lb spinach, trimmed and washed
1 kg/2 lb parsnips, peeled and chopped	2 lb parsnips, peeled and chopped
1 kg/2 lb carrots, chopped	2 lb carrots, chopped
3 eggs	3 eggs
2 tablespoons fresh wholewheat breadcrumbs	2 tablespoons soft wholewheat bread crumbs
2 tablespoons grated Parmesan cheese	2 tablespoons grated Parmesan cheese
1 tablespoon chopped fresh parsley to garnish	1 tablespoon chopped fresh parsley to garnish
White sauce:	**White sauce:**
50 g/2 oz butter	¼ cup butter
50 g/2 oz plain flour	½ cup all-purpose flour
420 ml/¾ pint milk	1¾ cups milk
salt	salt
freshly ground black pepper	freshly ground black pepper

Cook the spinach in a very little boiling salted water for about 7 minutes, until tender. Drain and chop. Cook the parsnips in boiling salted water for about 25 minutes, until very tender, and cook the carrots separately in boiling salted water for about 30 minutes, until very tender. Drain the parsnips and carrots.

To make the white sauce, melt the butter in a small saucepan, stir in the flour and cook, stirring, for 1 minute. Remove from the heat, gradually add the milk, then bring to the boil, stirring continuously. Season with salt and pepper. Place the three types of vegetables in three separate bowls and divide the sauce between them. Add an egg to each and beat well. This may be done in a food processor or blender, if preferred.

Pour the spinach mixture into a greased 20 cm/ 8 inch square ovenproof dish and cover with the parsnip mixture, then the carrot mixture. Combine the breadcrumbs and Parmesan and sprinkle over the top. Stand the dish in a bain marie and bake in a preheated moderate oven (180°C/350°F, Gas Mark 4) for 35 minutes. Sprinkle with parsley and serve immediately.
Serves 8

Stuffed Marrow (Squash)

METRIC/IMPERIAL	AMERICAN
1 medium marrow, halved lengthwise and seeded	1 medium squash, halved lengthwise and seeded
salt	salt
freshly ground black pepper	freshly ground black pepper
2 tablespoons olive oil	2 tablespoons olive oil
grilled bacon rashers to garnish (optional)	broiled bacon slices to garnish (optional)
Stuffing:	**Stuffing:**
50 g/2 oz butter	¼ cup butter
2 medium onions, sliced	2 medium onions, sliced
2 garlic cloves, chopped	2 garlic cloves, chopped
225 g/8 oz button mushrooms, sliced	2 cups button mushrooms, sliced
100 g/4 oz cooked long-grain rice	1 cup cooked long-grain rice
½ teaspoon grated nutmeg	½ teaspoon grated nutmeg
½ teaspoon ground cumin	½ teaspoon ground cumin
½ teaspoon ground coriander	½ teaspoon ground coriander
1 teaspoon dried basil	1 teaspoon dried basil
1 tablespoon chopped fresh parsley	1 tablespoon chopped fresh parsley
salt	salt
freshly ground black pepper	freshly ground black pepper

Blanch the marrow (squash) in boiling salted water in a large saucepan for 5 minutes, then drain well. Place both halves in a greased baking tin (pan) and sprinkle with salt and pepper.

To make the stuffing, melt the butter in a frying pan (skillet) over a low heat and gently sauté the onions and garlic for 5 minutes. Add the mushrooms, cook for another 5 minutes, then add the cooked rice and the spices. Add the herbs, season with salt and pepper and mix well together. Pile the mixture into the marrow (squash) halves, sprinkle with oil and bake in a preheated moderate oven (160°C/325°F, Gas Mark 3) for 45 minutes. Garnish with bacon, if liked.
Serves 6 to 8

Stuffed Peppers

METRIC/IMPERIAL	AMERICAN
4 large peppers	4 large peppers
50 g/2 oz butter	¼ cup butter
1 medium onion, sliced	1 medium onion, sliced
1 garlic clove, chopped	1 garlic clove, chopped
1 celery stick, sliced	1 stalk celery, sliced
50 g/2 oz button mushrooms, sliced	½ cup button mushrooms, sliced
225 g/8 oz cooked brown rice	1½ cups cooked brown rice
salt	salt
freshly ground black pepper	freshly ground black pepper
1 teaspoon dried basil	1 teaspoon dried basil
½ teaspoon paprika	½ teaspoon paprika

Cut the tops off the peppers and remove the cores and seeds. Blanch the peppers and the tops in boiling salted water for 5 minutes, then drain. Melt the butter in a large saucepan and sauté the onion, garlic and celery for 5 minutes, then add the mushrooms. Cook together for a further 5 minutes, then add the rice, salt, pepper, basil and paprika. Stir well and remove from the heat.

Stand the peppers upright in a greased ovenproof dish and stuff them with the rice mixture. Replace the pepper tops. Bake in a preheated moderate oven (160°C/325°F, Gas Mark 3) for 30 minutes. Serve immediately or allow to cool and serve cold with salad.
Serves 4

Variation: Add any minced (ground) leftover meat, such as beef or chicken, to the stuffing.

Spinach Soufflé

METRIC/IMPERIAL	AMERICAN
450 g/1 lb spinach, washed	1 lb spinach, washed
50 g/2 oz butter	¼ cup butter
50 g/2 oz plain flour	½ cup all-purpose flour
300 ml/½ pint milk	1¼ cups milk
50 g/2 oz Cheddar cheese, grated	½ cup shredded Cheddar cheese
salt	salt
freshly ground black pepper	freshly ground black pepper
4 eggs, separated	4 eggs, separated
sliced tomato to garnish	sliced tomato to garnish

Remove the stalks from the spinach and cook the leaves in a very little boiling salted water in a large saucepan for about 5 minutes, until tender. Drain and chop finely.

Melt the butter in a saucepan over a low heat. Stir in the flour and cook for 1 to 2 minutes, stirring. Remove from the heat and gradually add the milk, stirring all the time. Bring to the boil, then reduce the heat, stir in the cheese and cook for another minute. Season with salt and pepper. Remove from the heat and allow to cool. Whisk the egg whites until stiff.

Add the egg yolks and the spinach to the cheese sauce and mix well together. For a finer purée, mix together in a food processor or blender. Fold the spinach mixture into the egg whites and pour into a greased soufflé dish that is 15 cm/6 inches in diameter and 8.5 cm/3½ inches deep. Bake in a preheated moderately hot oven (190°C/375°F, Gas Mark 5) for 45 minutes or until well risen and golden brown. Garnish with tomato slices and serve immediately.
Serves 4

Vegetable Hot Pot

METRIC/IMPERIAL	AMERICAN
50 g/2 oz butter	¼ cup butter
2 medium onions, sliced	2 medium onions, sliced
2 parsnips, peeled and sliced	2 parsnips, peeled and sliced
3 small turnips, peeled and sliced	3 small turnips, peeled and sliced
2 courgettes, sliced	2 zucchini, sliced
100 g/4 oz button mushrooms	1 cup button mushrooms
600 ml/1 pint carrot juice or vegetable stock	2½ cups carrot juice or vegetable stock
1 small cauliflower, broken into florets	1 small cauliflower, broken into florets
salt	salt
freshly ground black pepper	freshly ground black pepper
dash of Tabasco sauce	dash of hot pepper sauce
6 slices fried bread, halved diagonally, to garnish	6 slices fried bread, halved diagonally, to garnish

Melt the butter in a heavy saucepan over a low heat and gently sauté the onions. Add the parsnips and turnips, cover and cook slowly for 10 minutes. Add the courgettes (zucchini), mushrooms and carrot juice or stock and bring slowly to the boil. Add the cauliflower florets and cook over a low heat for a further 30 minutes. Season to taste with salt, pepper and a dash of Tabasco (hot pepper) sauce. Alternatively, transfer to an ovenproof dish and cook in a preheated moderate oven (180°C/350°F, Gas Mark 4) for 30 minutes. Garnish with fried bread triangles and serve piping hot with buttered rice.
Serves 8

VEGETABLE SALADS

A salad can be substantial enough to serve as a lunch or supper dish, or it can be a delicate affair to serve as a dinner party starter. Whichever type you choose, make it as interesting as you can – vary textures, combine traditional and unlikely ingredients, and experiment with dressings.

Herby Green Salad

Use as many of the salad ingredients listed below as are available.

METRIC/IMPERIAL	AMERICAN
1 garlic clove, halved	1 garlic clove, halved
1 cos lettuce	1 romaine lettuce, washed
100 g/4 oz lamb's lettuce	¼ lb lamb's lettuce
1 bunch watercress	1 bunch watercress
1 punnet mustard and cress	1 box mustard and cress
1 bunch rocket	1 bunch rocket
1 bunch chives	1 bunch chives
1 bunch parsley	1 bunch parsley
1 bunch basil	1 bunch basil
1 bunch mint	1 bunch mint
2 oranges, peeled, sliced and quartered	2 oranges, peeled, sliced and quartered
Dressing:	**Dressing:**
2 tablespoons olive oil	2 tablespoons olive oil
1 tablespoon wine vinegar	1 tablespoon wine vinegar
1 tablespoon lemon juice	1 tablespoon lemon juice
2 garlic cloves, crushed	2 garlic cloves, crushed
1 teaspoon brown sugar	1 teaspoon brown sugar
1 teaspoon tarragon mustard	1 teaspoon tarragon mustard

Use the cut garlic clove to rub round the inside of a large salad bowl, then discard. Wash and prepare the salad greens. Chop the chives and parsley and strip the leaves from the basil and mint, discarding the stems. Place the salad greens and herbs in the salad bowl with the orange pieces and mix well.

To make the dressing, place all the ingredients in a bowl and whisk together, or place in a screw-topped jar and shake well. Pour over the salad and toss well just before serving.
Serves 8

Waldorf Salad

METRIC/IMPERIAL	AMERICAN
100 g/4 oz white cabbage, shredded	1½ cups shredded white cabbage
100 g/4 oz carrots, grated	1 cup grated carrots
2 celery sticks, chopped	2 stalks celery, chopped
2 red dessert apples, cored and sliced	2 red dessert apples, cored and sliced
50 g/2 oz walnuts, chopped	½ cup chopped walnuts
chopped fresh parsley to garnish	chopped fresh parsley to garnish
Dressing:	**Dressing:**
1 tablespoon olive oil	1 tablespoon olive oil
2 tablespoons plain yogurt	2 tablespoons plain yogurt
1 teaspoon lemon juice	1 teaspoon lemon juice
salt	salt
freshly ground black pepper	freshly ground black pepper

Combine the cabbage, carrot, celery, apple and walnuts in a salad bowl. To make the dressing, whisk all the ingredients together in a small bowl, or place in a screw-topped jar and shake well. Pour over the salad, toss well and garnish with chopped parsley.
Serves 8

Herby Green Salad

Variation: Add small pieces of cold chicken.

Three Bean Salad

METRIC/IMPERIAL	AMERICAN
2 medium onions, chopped	2 medium onions, chopped
2 celery sticks, chopped	2 stalks celery, chopped
2 tomatoes, chopped	2 tomatoes, chopped
225 g/8 oz broad beans, shelled and boiled	½ lb lima beans, shelled and boiled
175 g/6 oz dried red kidney beans or 1 × 400 g/14 oz can red kidney beans, drained	6 oz dried red kidney beans or 1 × 14 oz can red kidney beans, drained
175 g/6 oz dried black-eye beans or 1 × 14 oz can black-eye beans, drained	6 oz dried black-eye beans, or 1 × 14 oz can black-eye beans, drained
Dressing:	**Dressing:**
2 tablespoons olive oil	2 tablespoons olive oil
1 tablespoon wine vinegar	1 tablespoon wine vinegar
1 tablespoon lemon juice	1 tablespoon lemon juice
1 teaspoon coarse-grain mustard	1 teaspoon coarse-grain mustard
salt	salt
freshly ground black pepper	freshly ground black pepper
1 tablespoon chopped fresh basil	1 tablespoon chopped fresh basil

If using dried beans, soak them overnight, or for at least 6 to 8 hours, keeping the 2 types separate. Drain, then boil the red kidney beans rapidly in fresh water for 10 minutes to destroy harmful toxins. Simmer for 1½ to 2 hours. Drain the black-eye beans and, in a separate pan, bring to the boil in fresh water and simmer for 1½ to 2 hours. Drain well.

Combine all the salad ingredients in a large earthenware bowl. To make the dressing, place all the ingredients in a bowl and whisk together, or place in a screw-topped jar and shake well. Pour over the salad and toss thoroughly. Leave in the refrigerator for at least 1 hour before serving.
Serves 6

Mexican Salad

METRIC/IMPERIAL	AMERICAN
175 g/6 oz dried butter beans or 1 × 400 g/14 oz can butter beans, drained	1 cup dried butter beans or 1 × 14 oz can butter beans, drained
1 green pepper, cored, seeded and chopped	1 green pepper, cored, seeded and chopped
1 red pepper, cored, seeded and chopped	1 red pepper, cored, seeded and chopped
1 hot button pepper, finely chopped	1 hot button pepper, finely chopped
4 medium tomatoes, chopped	4 medium tomatoes, chopped
2 medium onions, chopped	2 medium onions, chopped
2 garlic cloves, crushed	2 garlic cloves, crushed
2 tablespoons chopped fresh parsley	2 tablespoons chopped fresh parsley
Dressing:	**Dressing:**
2 tablespoons olive oil	2 tablespoons olive oil
1 tablespoon wine vinegar	1 tablespoon wine vinegar
1 tablespoon lemon juice	1 tablespoon lemon juice
1 teaspoon brown sugar	1 teaspoon brown sugar
salt	salt
freshly ground black pepper	freshly ground black pepper
dash of Tabasco sauce	dash of hot pepper sauce

If using dried butter beans, soak them in plenty of cold water overnight or for at least 6 to 8 hours. Drain them and place in a saucepan with plenty of fresh water and bring to the boil. Cover the pan and reduce heat. Simmer for 1½ to 2 hours. Drain.

Place all the salad ingredients in a salad bowl and mix well. To make the dressing, place all the ingredients in a bowl and whisk well together, or place in a screw-topped jar and shake well. Pour over the salad, toss thoroughly and leave in the refrigerator to marinate for at least 1 hour before serving.
Serves 8

Variation: Add chopped garlic sausage.

Mushroom and Lemon Salad

METRIC/IMPERIAL	AMERICAN
1 lemon	1 lemon
450 g/1 lb button mushrooms, sliced	4 cups button mushrooms, sliced
squeeze of lemon juice	squeeze of lemon juice
Dressing:	**Dressing:**
2 tablespoons olive oil	2 tablespoons olive oil
1 tablespoon wine vinegar	1 tablespoon wine vinegar
1 tablespoon lemon juice	1 tablespoon lemon juice
1 teaspoon coriander seeds	1 teaspoon coriander seeds
1 tablespoon chopped fresh parsley	1 tablespoon chopped fresh parsley

Trim off the ends of the lemon and cut the remainder into very thin slices. Chop these slices finely. Place the mushrooms in a salad bowl with the lemon. Mix well and sprinkle with lemon juice. To make the dressing, place all the ingredients in a bowl and whisk together, or place in a screw-topped jar and shake well. Pour over the salad and mix thoroughly. Leave in the refrigerator to marinate for about 1 hour before serving.
Serves 6

Caesar Salad

A Caesar Salad should be made just before it is going to be served, ideally in front of your guests. If you do this, break the egg straight into the salad without beating it.

METRIC/IMPERIAL	AMERICAN
1 egg, beaten (see introduction)	1 egg, beaten (see introduction)
1 cos lettuce, washed and dried	1 romaine lettuce, washed and dried
50 g/2 oz grated Parmesan cheese	½ cup grated Parmesan cheese
4 tablespoons croûtons (see page 7)	4 tablespoons croûtons (see page 7)
Dressing:	**Dressing:**
2 tablespoons olive oil	2 tablespoons olive oil
1 tablespoon wine vinegar	1 tablespoon wine vinegar
1 tablespoon lemon juice	1 tablespoon lemon juice
1 teaspoon brown sugar	1 teaspoon brown sugar
1 garlic clove, crushed	1 garlic clove, crushed
salt	salt
freshly ground black pepper	freshly ground black pepper

To make the dressing, place all the ingredients in a bowl and whisk together, or place in a screw-topped jar and shake well.

Roughly tear the lettuce leaves apart (do not cut them), and place them in a large wooden salad bowl. Add the egg, Parmesan and the croûtons. Pour the dressing over the salad and toss thoroughly. The secret of a Caesar Salad is in the mixing. Serve immediately.
Serves 6 to 8

Health Food Salad

METRIC/IMPERIAL	AMERICAN
225 g/8 oz wholewheat grain, soaked overnight and drained	1 cup wholewheat grain, soaked overnight and drained
100 g/4 oz raisins	⅔ cup raisins
100 g/4 oz chopped walnuts	1 cup chopped walnuts
1 red dessert apple, cored and chopped	1 red dessert apple, cored and chopped
1 orange, peeled and sliced	1 orange, peeled and sliced
225 g/8 oz bean sprouts	4 cups bean sprouts
Dressing:	**Dressing:**
2 tablespoons olive oil	2 tablespoons olive oil
1 tablespoon wine vinegar	1 tablespoon wine vinegar
1 tablespoon lemon juice	1 tablespoon lemon juice
1 garlic clove, crushed	1 garlic clove, crushed
salt	salt
freshly ground black pepper	freshly ground black pepper
To garnish:	**To garnish:**
bunch of watercress	bunch of watercress
roasted peanuts	roasted peanuts

Place the wholewheat in a large saucepan, cover with fresh cold salted water and bring to the boil. Reduce the heat and simmer gently for 1½ hours, until tender. Drain and allow to cool.

When the wholewheat is cold, place in a salad bowl with the raisins, walnuts, apple, orange and bean sprouts and mix well. To make the dressing, place all the ingredients in a bowl and whisk together, or place in a screw-topped jar and shake well. Pour over the salad and toss. Garnish with watercress and peanuts and serve immediately.
Serves 8

Potato Salad

METRIC/IMPERIAL	AMERICAN
1 kg/2 lb old potatoes, peeled	2 lb old potatoes, peeled
½ cucumber, peeled and chopped	½ cucumber, peeled and chopped
1 medium onion, sliced	1 medium onion, sliced
250 ml/8 fl oz mayonnaise	1 cup mayonnaise
120 ml/4 fl oz plain yogurt	½ cup plain yogurt
salt	salt
freshly ground black pepper	freshly ground black pepper
Garnish:	**Garnish:**
2 hard-boiled eggs, sliced	2 hard-cooked eggs, sliced
a few small mint leaves	a few small mint leaves

Cook the potatoes in boiling salted water for 15 to 20 minutes, until tender. Drain and allow to cool, then chop roughly. Combine the potatoes, cucumber and onion with the mayonnaise and the yogurt and season to taste with salt and pepper.

Garnish with slices of egg and a few small mint leaves.
Serves 8

Dandelion Salad

METRIC/IMPERIAL	AMERICAN
450 g/1 lb young dandelion leaves, washed	1 lb young dandelion leaves, washed
1 garlic clove, halved	1 garlic clove, halved
100 g/4 oz streaky bacon	6 streaky bacon slices
4 tablespoons croûtons (see page 7)	4 tablespoons croûtons (see page 7)
Dressing:	**Dressing:**
2 tablespoons olive oil	2 tablespoons olive oil
1 tablespoon white wine vinegar	1 tablespoon white wine vinegar
1 tablespoon lemon juice	1 tablespoon lemon juice
salt	salt
freshly ground black pepper	freshly ground black pepper

Select young dandelion leaves very carefully. Use the cut garlic clove to rub round the inside of a wooden salad bowl, then discard. Grill (broil) the bacon, cool, then roughly chop. To make the dressing, whisk all the ingredients together in a bowl, or place in a screw-topped jar and shake well. Combine the dandelion leaves, bacon and croûtons in the salad bowl. Just before serving, pour over the dressing and mix thoroughly.
Serves 6

Fruity Cabbage Salad

METRIC/IMPERIAL	AMERICAN
450 g/1 lb white cabbage, finely shredded	1 lb white cabbage, finely chopped
50 g/2 oz dried apricots, finely chopped	⅓ cup finely chopped dried apricots
75 g/3 oz raisins	½ cup raisins
4 spring onions, chopped	4 scallions, chopped
1 green pepper, cored, seeded and chopped	1 green pepper, cored, seeded and chopped
½ bunch radishes, sliced	½ bunch radishes, sliced
Dressing:	**Dressing:**
150 g/5 oz plain yogurt	⅔ cup plain yogurt
2 teaspoons French mustard	2 teaspoons Dijon-style mustard
1 garlic clove, crushed	1 garlic clove, crushed
1 tablespoon clear honey	1 tablespoon clear honey
salt	salt
freshly ground black pepper	freshly ground black pepper

Place all the salad ingredients in a large bowl and mix well. To make the dressing, whisk all the ingredients together in a small bowl, or place in a screw-topped jar and shake well. Pour over the salad just before serving and toss well.
Serves 6 to 8

Carrot and Raisin Salad

METRIC/IMPERIAL	AMERICAN
450 g/1 lb carrots, grated	4 cups grated carrot
75 g/3 oz raisins	½ cup raisins
4 tablespoons soured cream	4 tablespoons sour cream
25 g/1 oz hazelnuts, roughly chopped	¼ cup roughly chopped hazelnuts
salt	salt
freshly ground black pepper	freshly ground black pepper
snipped chives or chopped parsley to garnish	snipped chives or chopped parsley to garnish

Mix together the carrot and raisins in a serving bowl. Mix the soured cream, hazelnuts, salt and pepper. Pour this mixture over the carrots just before serving. Sprinkle with chives or parsley.
Serves 4 to 6

Fruity Cabbage Salad
Carrot and Raisin Salad
(Photograph: The Californian Raisin Advisory Board)

Sweet and Sour Salad

METRIC/IMPERIAL	AMERICAN
½ red cabbage, chopped	½ red cabbage, chopped
3 heads chicory, chopped	3 heads endive, chopped
1 orange, peeled and sliced	1 orange, peeled and sliced
1 mango, peeled and sliced	1 mango, peeled and sliced
1 grapefruit, peeled and sliced	1 grapefruit, peeled and sliced
1 red apple, cored and sliced	1 red apple, cored and sliced
2 tablespoons flaked almonds, toasted, to garnish	2 tablespoons slivered almonds, toasted, to garnish
Dressing:	**Dressing:**
2 tablespoons olive oil	2 tablespoons olive oil
1 tablespoon wine vinegar	1 tablespoon wine vinegar
1 tablespoon lime or lemon juice	1 tablespoon lime or lemon juice
1 garlic clove, crushed	1 garlic clove, crushed
1 tablespoon chopped fresh parsley	1 tablespoon chopped fresh parsley

Combine the salad ingredients in a large bowl. Mix well. To make the dressing, place all the ingredients in a bowl and whisk together, or place in a screw-topped jar and shake well. Pour over the salad and toss well just before serving. Garnish with almonds.
Serves 8

Tabouleh Salad

METRIC/IMPERIAL	AMERICAN
450 g/1 lb cracked wheat	3½ cups cracked wheat
6 spring onions, chopped	6 scallions, chopped
2 garlic cloves, chopped	2 garlic cloves, chopped
bunch of fresh parsley, chopped	bunch of fresh parsley, chopped
bunch of fresh mint, chopped	bunch of fresh mint, chopped
grated rind and juice of 2 lemons	grated rind and juice of 2 lemons
salt	salt
freshly ground black pepper	freshly ground black pepper
2 tablespoons olive oil	2 tablespoons olive oil
To garnish:	**To garnish:**
12 black olives	12 ripe olives
1 red pepper, cored, seeded and chopped	1 red pepper, cored, seeded and chopped

Place the cracked wheat in a large bowl, cover with plenty of cold water and leave to soak for 1 hour,
stirring occasionally. Taking a handful of the wheat at a time, squeeze out the water and spread on kitchen paper towels. Allow to dry.

Combine the cracked wheat, spring onions (scallions), garlic, parsley and mint in a salad bowl. Mix thoroughly and add the lemon rind and juice, salt, pepper and oil. Mix again, taste and correct the seasoning if necessary. Garnish with olives and red pepper.
Serves 12

Note: It is important to have plenty of parsley and mint in this salad. Such large quantities may be more easily chopped in a food processor or blender.

Spinach Salad

METRIC/IMPERIAL	AMERICAN
450 g/1 lb fresh young spinach, washed	1 lb fresh young spinach, washed
6 spring onions, chopped	6 scallions, chopped
1 red dessert apple, cored and chopped	1 red dessert apple, cored and chopped
2 hard-boiled eggs, chopped	2 hard-cooked eggs, chopped
Dressing:	**Dressing:**
2 tablespoons olive oil	2 tablespoons olive oil
1 tablespoon wine vinegar	1 tablespoon wine vinegar
1 tablespoon lemon juice	1 tablespoon lemon juice
6 fresh basil leaves, chopped	6 fresh basil leaves, chopped
1 garlic clove, crushed	1 garlic clove, crushed
To garnish:	**To garnish:**
4 tablespoons wholewheat croûtons (see page 7)	4 tablespoons wholewheat croûtons (see page 7)
4 tablespoons sunflower seeds	4 tablespoons sunflower seeds

Remove the stalk and centre vein from each spinach leaf. Place the leaves in a salad bowl with the spring onions (scallions), apple and chopped eggs. To make the dressing, place the ingredients in a bowl and whisk together, or place in a screw-topped jar and shake well. Just before serving, pour the dressing over the salad and toss well. Garnish with croûtons and sunflower seeds.
Serves 8

Variation: Add 100 g/4 oz (¼ lb) crumbled crisp-fried streaky (fatty) bacon.

Chinese Salad

METRIC/IMPERIAL	AMERICAN
1 Chinese cabbage, washed and chopped	1 Chinese cabbage, washed and chopped
4 medium spring onions, chopped	4 medium scallions, chopped
225 g/8 oz bean sprouts	4 cups bean sprouts
225 g/8 oz mange-tout, cooked	½ lb snow peas, cooked
2 fresh peaches or canned peach slices	2 fresh peaches or canned peach slices
Dressing:	**Dressing:**
4 tablespoons olive oil	4 tablespoons olive oil
2 tablespoons wine vinegar	2 tablespoons wine vinegar
1 tablespoon soy sauce	1 tablespoon soy sauce
juice of 1 lime or lemon	juice of 1 lime or lemon
salt	salt
freshly ground black pepper	freshly ground black pepper

Combine the cabbage, spring onions (scallions), bean sprouts and mange-tout (snow peas) in a large delicate bowl. To make the dressing, place all the ingredients in a bowl and whisk together, or place in a screw-topped jar and shake well. Pour over the salad, toss lightly and garnish with sliced peaches. Serve immediately.
Serves 12

Variation: Stir in 100 g/4 oz (⅔ cup) peeled prawns (shelled shrimp) before garnishing with peaches.

Sprouting Salad

METRIC/IMPERIAL	AMERICAN
1 garlic clove, halved	1 garlic clove, halved
100 g/4 oz bean sprouts	2 cups bean sprouts
100 g/4 oz alfalfa sprouts	2 cups alfalfa sprouts
100 g/4 oz green lentil sprouts	2 cups green lentil sprouts
100 g/4 oz cashew nuts	1 cup cashew nuts
1 large tomato, chopped	1 large tomato, chopped
4 spring onions, sliced	4 scallions, sliced
2 tablespoons wholewheat garlic croûtons (see page 7) to garnish	2 tablespoons wholewheat garlic croûtons (see page 7) to garnish
Dressing:	**Dressing:**
2 tablespoons olive oil	2 tablespoons olive oil
1 tablespoon soy sauce	1 tablespoon soy sauce
1 tablespoon lemon juice	1 tablespoon lemon juice
1 garlic clove, crushed	1 garlic clove, crushed
salt	salt
freshly ground black pepper	freshly ground black pepper

Use the cut garlic to rub round the inside of a large salad bowl, then discard. Combine all the salad ingredients, except the croûtons, in the bowl and mix together. To make the dressing, whisk all the ingredients together in a small bowl, or place in a screw-topped jar and shake well. Just before serving, pour over the salad and toss thoroughly. Garnish with croûtons.
Serves 8

Avocado, Mozzarella and Tomato Salad

METRIC/IMPERIAL	AMERICAN
2 avocados, stoned, peeled and sliced lengthwise	2 avocados, pitted, peeled and sliced lengthwise
225 g/8 oz Mozzarella cheese, sliced	½ lb Mozzarella cheese, sliced
4 beef tomatoes, sliced	4 beef tomatoes, sliced
bunch of fresh basil	bunch of fresh basil
French bread and butter to serve	French bread and butter to serve
Dressing:	**Dressing:**
2 tablespoons olive oil	2 tablespoons olive oil
1 tablespoon wine vinegar	1 tablespoon wine vinegar
1 tablespoon lemon juice	1 tablespoon lemon juice
1 teaspoon brown sugar	1 teaspoon brown sugar
1 garlic clove, crushed	1 garlic clove, crushed
salt	salt
freshly ground black pepper	freshly ground black pepper

Arrange the avocado slices in a line down the centre of a serving platter, interleaving each slice with half a slice of Mozzarella cheese. Arrange the tomato slices in lines on either side. Scatter basil leaves over the salad, tearing any that are very large. To make the dressing, place all the ingredients in a bowl and whisk together, or place in a screw-topped jar and shake well. Sprinkle the dressing over the salad and serve immediately with French bread and butter.
Serves 8

SIDE DISHES

Make more of vegetables, don't just boil them and serve them plain. Combine the vegetables that are available to create interesting vegetable side dishes to complement and enhance the main meal.

Chinese Stir-fried Vegetables

METRIC/IMPERIAL	AMERICAN
1 tablespoon oil	1 tablespoon oil
50 g/2 oz streaky bacon, derinded and chopped	¼ cup chopped fatty bacon
1 large onion, peeled and chopped	1 large onion, peeled and chopped
1 garlic clove, peeled and crushed	1 garlic clove, peeled and crushed
1 tablespoon peeled and grated fresh root ginger	1 tablespoon peeled and grated fresh ginger root
50 g/2 oz mushrooms, sliced	½ cup sliced mushrooms
450 g/1 lb mange-tout, topped and tailed	1 lb snow peas, topped and tailed
450 g/1 lb Chinese or other cabbage, shredded	6 cups shredded Chinese or other cabbage
100 g/4 oz bean sprouts	2 cups bean sprouts
50 g/2 oz whole peanuts, shelled	¼ cup whole shelled peanuts
1 tablespoon soy sauce	1 tablespoon soy sauce
5 tablespoons stock or water	⅓ cup stock or water
salt	salt
freshly ground black pepper	freshly ground black pepper

Heat the oil in a wok or large frying pan (skillet). Add the bacon, onion, garlic, ginger and mushrooms and fry briskly for 3 minutes, stirring constantly.

Add the mange-tout (snow peas) and cabbage and fry for a further 2 minutes, stirring constantly.

Add the remaining ingredients and stir-fry over moderate heat for about 5 minutes until the vegetables are tender but still crisp, and most of the liquid has evaporated. Taste and adjust the seasoning and serve immediately.
Serves 4

Red Cabbage and Pine Nuts

METRIC/IMPERIAL	AMERICAN
50 g/2 oz butter	¼ cup butter
1 medium onion, sliced	1 medium onion, sliced
2 garlic cloves, chopped	2 garlic cloves, chopped
½ red cabbage, chopped	½ red cabbage, chopped
2 medium dessert apples, cored and chopped	2 medium dessert apples, cored and chopped
50 g/2 oz pine nuts	½ cup pine nuts
50 g/2 oz raisins	¼ cup raisins
300 ml/½ pint dry cider	1¼ cups hard cider
1 teaspoon salt	1 teaspoon salt
½ teaspoon grated nutmeg	½ teaspoon grated nutmeg
1 teaspoon mixed spice	1 teaspoon ground allspice
1 teaspoon ground ginger	1 teaspoon ground ginger
freshly ground black pepper	freshly ground black pepper

Melt the butter in a heavy saucepan or pressure cooker and sauté the onion and garlic until just translucent. Add the chopped red cabbage, cover and cook gently for 10 minutes, stirring occasionally. Add the apple, pine nuts, raisins, cider, salt, nutmeg, spice, ginger and pepper and cook gently over a low heat for 40 minutes. If using a pressure cooker, bring to high pressure and cook for 5 minutes. Remove from the heat and allow the pressure to reduce at room temperature.
Serves 8

Chinese Stir-fried Vegetables

Minted New Potatoes, Carrots and Peas

METRIC/IMPERIAL	AMERICAN
450 g/1 lb small new potatoes	1 lb small new potatoes
450 g/1 lb small new carrots	1 lb small new carrots
450 g/1 lb new peas, shelled	1 lb new peas, shelled
bunch of fresh mint	bunch of fresh mint
To garnish:	**To garnish:**
50 g/2 oz butter	¼ cup butter
1 tablespoon chopped fresh parsley	1 tablespoon chopped fresh parsley

If the potatoes and the carrots are very young it should not be necessary to scrape them; just wash under running water. Cook the potatoes, carrots and peas in enough boiling salted water to cover in three separate saucepans. Add a sprig of mint to each saucepan. Cook the potatoes for about 10 minutes or until just tender. Cook the carrots for about 6 minutes, depending on size, until just tender. Finally, cook the peas for about 6 minutes until just tender. Drain all the vegetables and combine in a warmed vegetable dish. Dot with butter and sprinkle with chopped parsley.
Serves 8

Candied Sweet Potatoes

METRIC/IMPERIAL	AMERICAN
1 kg/2 lb sweet potatoes, scrubbed	2 lb sweet potatoes, scrubbed
25 g/1 oz butter	2 tablespoons butter
2 tablespoons single cream	2 tablespoons light cream
1 egg	1 egg
salt	salt
freshly ground black pepper	freshly ground black pepper
12 white marshmallows	12 white marshmallows
1 tablespoon brown sugar	1 tablespoon brown sugar

Cook the sweet potatoes in their skins in boiling salted water for 20 to 30 minutes, until tender. Drain and allow to cool slightly. Peel the potatoes and place in a large bowl with the butter, cream and egg. Season to taste with salt and pepper and mash well with a fork. Place in an ovenproof dish, top with the marshmallows and sprinkle with the sugar. Bake in a preheated hot oven (220°C/425°F, Gas Mark 7) for about 20 minutes, until the marshmallows have melted and are candied on top. Serve piping hot.
Serves 8

Fennel and Apple in Cider

METRIC/IMPERIAL	AMERICAN
2 bulbs fennel, trimmed and quartered	2 bulbs fennel, trimmed and quartered
1 large cooking apple, peeled, cored and sliced	1 large tart apple, peeled, cored and sliced
300 ml/½ pint dry cider	1¼ cups hard cider
2 tablespoons raisins	2 tablespoons raisins
salt	salt
freshly ground black pepper	freshly ground black pepper
2 tablespoons chopped fresh parsley to garnish	2 tablespoons chopped fresh parsley to garnish

Combine the fennel and apple in a casserole with a lid. Pour on the cider and sprinkle with the raisins, salt and pepper. Cover and bake in a moderately hot oven (190°C/375°F, Gas Mark 5) for about 45 minutes or until the fennel is tender but still retains its shape. Drain off the cider into a saucepan and boil rapidly to reduce it. Then pour back over the apple and fennel. Serve garnished with chopped parsley.
Serves 8

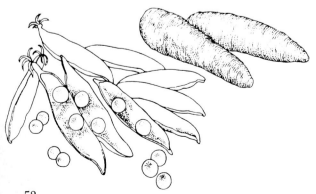

Courgettes (Zucchini) Provençal

METRIC/IMPERIAL	AMERICAN
15 g/½ oz butter	1 tablespoon butter
1 tablespoon olive oil	1 tablespoon olive oil
2 medium onions, sliced	2 medium onions, sliced
2 garlic cloves, chopped	2 garlic cloves, chopped
6 courgettes, thinly sliced	6 zucchini, thinly sliced
1 large tomato, chopped	1 large tomato, chopped
1 teaspoon chopped fresh basil	1 teaspoon chopped fresh basil
1 teaspoon chopped fresh chives	1 teaspoon chopped fresh chives
salt	salt
freshly ground black pepper	freshly ground black pepper
12 black olives, stoned (optional)	12 pitted ripe olives (optional)

Heat the butter and the olive oil in a heavy saucepan, add the onions and garlic and sauté until just translucent. Add the courgettes (zucchini) and combine well. Add the tomatoes, herbs, salt, pepper and olives, if desired, cover and cook for 15 minutes or until the courgettes (zucchini) are tender but still slightly crisp. Serve immediately.
Serves 4

Variation: Add 100 g/4 oz (⅔ cup) peeled prawns (shelled shrimp) 1 to 2 minutes before serving.

Italian-style Peas

METRIC/IMPERIAL	AMERICAN
4 tablespoons oil	¼ cup oil
1 garlic clove, halved	1 garlic clove, halved
50 g/2 oz gammon, sliced into fine strips	¼ cup fine strips of ham
400 g/14 oz shelled fresh or frozen peas	2½ cups shelled fresh or frozen peas
275 g/9 oz tomatoes, peeled and chopped	1 cup chopped, peeled tomatoes
salt	salt
freshly ground black pepper	freshly ground black pepper
To garnish:	**To garnish:**
1 basil sprig, chopped	1 basil sprig, chopped
1 tablespoon chopped parsley	1 tablespoon chopped parsley

Heat the oil in a pan. Add the garlic and fry until golden brown. Remove and discard the garlic. Add the gammon (ham), peas and tomatoes to the pan, mixing well. Season with salt and pepper to taste and cook, over a low heat, for about 10 to 15 minutes, adding a little water if necessary. Sprinkle with the basil and parsley before serving.
Serves 4

Haricot (Navy) Beans Burgundy-style

METRIC/IMPERIAL	AMERICAN
500 g/1 lb haricot beans, soaked overnight	1 lb navy beans, soaked overnight
600 ml/1 pint cold water	2½ cups cold water
½ sprig rosemary	½ sprig rosemary
2 shallots, finely sliced	2 shallots, finely sliced
1 bay leaf	1 bay leaf
1 × 64 g/2¼ oz can tomato purée	1 × 2¼ oz can tomato paste
1 tablespoon oil	1 tablespoon oil
125 g/4 oz bacon, derinded and chopped	½ cup chopped, derinded bacon
150 ml/¼ pint dry red wine	⅔ cup dry red wine
salt	salt
freshly ground black pepper	freshly ground black pepper
1 tablespoon chopped mixed herbs	1 tablespoon chopped mixed herbs

Drain the haricot (navy) beans and place in a pan with the water. Add the rosemary, bring slowly to the boil, then lower the heat, cover and cook gently for about 30 minutes.

Add the shallots, bay leaf and tomato purée (paste) and stir well. Cover and simmer over a low heat, for a further 20 to 30 minutes. Discard the rosemary sprig.

Meanwhile, heat the oil in a large pan. Add the bacon and fry until crisp and brown. Add the red wine and the beans with their cooking liquid. Season with salt and pepper to taste and cook for a further 5 minutes. Discard the bay leaf. Sprinkle with the herbs before serving.
Serves 6

Courgette (Zucchini) and Tomato with Basil

METRIC/IMPERIAL	AMERICAN
750 g/1½ lb courgettes, sliced	1½ lb zucchini, sliced
salt	salt
2 tablespoons olive oil	2 tablespoons olive oil
1 small onion, chopped	1 small onion, chopped
1 garlic clove, crushed	1 garlic clove, crushed
450 g/1 lb tomatoes, peeled and sliced	1 lb tomatoes, skinned and sliced
2 tablespoons wine vinegar	2 tablespoons wine vinegar
1 tablespoon lemon juice	1 tablespoon lemon juice
1 tablespoon caster sugar	1 tablespoon superfine sugar
1 tablespoon chopped fresh basil	1 tablespoon chopped fresh basil
freshly ground black pepper	freshly ground black pepper

Sprinkle the courgettes (zucchini) with salt and toss lightly. Leave to drain for 1 hour. Shake the courgettes (zucchini) in a cloth to dry. Heat the oil in a large frying pan (skillet) and sauté the onion and garlic for 5 minutes until soft. Add the courgettes (zucchini) and cook gently, stirring occasionally, for about 10 to 15 minutes. When they are soft, add the tomatoes. Stir in the vinegar, lemon juice, sugar and basil. Add salt and pepper to taste and cook for a further 5 minutes. Transfer to a warm serving dish and serve immediately.
Serves 4

Cabbage with Bacon

METRIC/IMPERIAL	AMERICAN
4 streaky bacon rashers, diced	4 fatty bacon slices, diced
1 garlic clove, crushed	1 garlic clove, crushed
1 sprig of rosemary	1 sprig of rosemary
1 medium savoy cabbage, shredded	1 medium savoy cabbage, shredded
150 ml/¼ pint chicken stock	⅔ cup chicken stock
salt	salt
freshly ground black pepper	freshly ground black pepper

Put the bacon, garlic and rosemary in a heavy based frying pan (skillet) and sauté over moderate heat for 5 minutes until browned. Lower the heat and add the cabbage, stock, salt and pepper to taste. Cover and cook gently for 40 minutes, stirring frequently. Transfer to a warmed serving dish and serve immediately.
Serves 4 to 6

Ratatouille

METRIC/IMPERIAL	AMERICAN
2 tablespoons olive oil	2 tablespoons olive oil
2 medium onions, sliced	2 medium onions, sliced
2 garlic cloves, chopped	2 garlic cloves, chopped
2 medium aubergines, chopped	2 medium eggplants, chopped
1 green pepper, cored, seeded and chopped	1 green pepper, cored, seeded and chopped
1 red pepper, cored, seeded and chopped	1 red pepper, cored, seeded and chopped
1 chilli, seeded and chopped	1 chili, seeded and chopped
3 courgettes, thinly sliced	3 zucchini, thinly sliced
1 × 750 g/1½ lb can of tomatoes	1 × 1½ lb can of tomatoes
1 teaspoon salt	1 teaspoon salt
freshly ground black pepper	freshly ground black pepper
1 teaspoon paprika	1 teaspoon paprika
dash of Tabasco sauce	dash of hot pepper sauce
1 teaspoon chopped fresh basil	1 teaspoon chopped fresh basil
1 teaspoon chopped fresh chives	1 teaspoon chopped fresh chives
1 tablespoon tomato purée	1 tablespoon tomato paste
1 teaspoon brown sugar	1 teaspoon brown sugar
50 g/2 oz grated Parmesan cheese to garnish	½ cup grated Parmesan cheese to garnish

Heat the oil in a large heavy frying pan (skillet) and sauté the onions and garlic together for about 5 minutes, until just translucent. Add the aubergine (eggplant), peppers and courgettes (zucchini), stir thoroughly and cook together for about 5 minutes. Add all the remaining ingredients, except the Parmesan, bring to the boil, then reduce the heat and simmer slowly for 45 minutes, stirring occasionally. Serve as a side dish, sprinkled with Parmesan.
Serves 8

Note: Served hot or cold, this dish also makes an excellent starter.

Courgette (Zucchini) and Tomato with Basil
Cabbage with Bacon

Mange-tout (Snow Peas), Orange and Almonds

METRIC/IMPERIAL	AMERICAN
450 g/1 lb mange-tout, topped and tailed	1 lb snow peas, topped and tailed
2 oranges, peeled and sliced	2 oranges, peeled and sliced
100 g/4 oz flaked almonds, toasted	1 cup slivered almonds, toasted
salt	salt
freshly ground black pepper	freshly ground black pepper
knob of butter to garnish	knob of butter to garnish

Cook the mange-tout (snow peas) in boiling salted water for about 5 minutes, until just cooked but still crisp. The time needed will vary according to the size of the mange-tout so test frequently. Drain well and transfer to a warmed vegetable serving dish.

Place the orange slices in a small saucepan and warm them slightly, then add to the mange-tout (snow peas) with the almonds, salt and pepper. Mix and serve immediately, garnished with a knob of butter.
Serves 8

Sweet and Sour Okra

METRIC/IMPERIAL	AMERICAN
450 g/1 lb small okra	1 lb small okra
2 tablespoons olive oil	2 tablespoons olive oil
1 medium onion, sliced	1 medium onion, sliced
2 garlic cloves, crushed	2 garlic cloves, crushed
4 whole cardamoms	4 whole cardamoms
grated rind and juice of 2 lemons	grated rind and juice of 2 lemons
2 tablespoons clear honey	2 tablespoons honey
1 teaspoon salt	1 teaspoon salt
1 teaspoon ground cumin	1 teaspoon ground cumin
1 orange, peeled and sliced to garnish	1 orange, peeled and sliced to garnish

Cut the stems from the okra without damaging the pod so that they remain intact during cooking. Heat the oil in a frying pan (skillet) and gently sauté the onion and garlic with the cardamoms for about 10 minutes, until just brown. Add all the remaining ingredients, except the orange, and simmer together for about 10 minutes or until the okra is just soft. Serve immediately, garnished with slices of orange.
Serves 4 to 6

Broad (Lima) Beans and Stilton

METRIC/IMPERIAL	AMERICAN
450 g/1 lb shelled broad beans	1 lb shelled lima beans
25 g/1 oz butter	2 tablespoons butter
50 g/2 oz crumbled Stilton cheese	½ cup crumbled Stilton cheese
salt	salt
freshly ground black pepper	freshly ground black pepper
1 tablespoon chopped fresh parsley to garnish	1 tablespoon chopped fresh parsley to garnish

Cook the broad beans (lima beans) in boiling salted water for about 7 minutes until just tender. Place in a warmed vegetable dish, top with the butter and the Stilton and garnish with chopped parsley.
Serves 6

Note: This makes an ideal vegetable side dish to serve with steak, or it can be turned into a meal in itself with a little chopped ham. Small broad beans (Lima beans) are more tender and tasty than large ones.
Serves 6

Turnip and Carrot Purée

METRIC/IMPERIAL
6 medium turnips, peeled and chopped
4 medium carrots, chopped
50 g/2 oz butter
salt
freshly ground black pepper
120 ml/4 fl oz single cream
50 g/2 oz flaked almonds, toasted, to garnish

AMERICAN
6 medium turnips, peeled and chopped
4 medium carrots, chopped
¼ cup butter
salt
freshly ground black pepper
½ cup light cream
½ cup slivered almonds, toasted, to garnish

Cook the turnips and carrots in boiling salted water for about 20 minutes, until nicely tender. Drain and place in a food processor or blender with the butter. Process for 1 minute. Season with salt and pepper, add the cream and process again briefly. Place in a warmed vegetable dish and sprinkle with almonds. Keep warm in the oven until ready to serve.
Serves 6

Purée of Brussels Sprouts

METRIC/IMPERIAL
1 kg/2 lb Brussels sprouts, trimmed
100 g/4 oz butter, softened
salt
freshly ground black pepper
To garnish:
1 egg yolk
1 tablespoon chopped fresh parsley

AMERICAN
2 lb Brussels sprouts, trimmed
½ cup butter, softened
salt
freshly ground black pepper
To garnish:
1 egg yolk
1 tablespoon chopped fresh parsley

Cook the Brussels sprouts in boiling salted water in a large saucepan for about 7 minutes, until just tender but still crisp. The time will vary according to the size of the Brussels sprouts, so test frequently. Drain the Brussels sprouts and place them in a food processor or blender with the butter and salt and pepper to taste. Process for 1 minute, then taste and correct the seasoning, if necessary. Place in a warmed vegetable dish and, just before serving, garnish with an egg yolk and sprinkle chopped parsley over the top.
Serves 8

Broccoli and Shallots with Black (Ripe) Olives

METRIC/IMPERIAL
450 g/1 lb broccoli spears, washed and trimmed
224 g/8 oz shallots, skinned
1 tablespoon olive oil
12 black olives, stoned
1 tablespoon lemon juice
salt
freshly ground black pepper

AMERICAN
1 lb broccoli spears, washed and trimmed
½ lb shallots, skinned
1 tablespoon olive oil
12 pitted ripe olives
1 tablespoon lemon juice
salt
freshly ground black pepper

Cook the broccoli spears in boiling salted water for about 7 minutes, until just tender but not soft. Drain well. Cook the shallots in boiling salted water for about 20 minutes, until tender. Drain well. Heat the oil in a large frying pan (skillet) and add the broccoli, shallots, olives and lemon juice and mix together. Season with salt and pepper to taste and serve immediately.
Serves 6

Variation: Add chopped, grilled (broiled) bacon rashers (slices). Alternatively, serve with steak or chops.

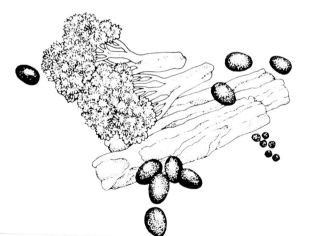

BREADS AND FRITTERS

Making bread can be a most rewarding experience, especially if you use ingredients like pumpkin that you would not expect to find in bread. Equally surprising and delicious are vegetable fritters.

Savoury Plait (Braid)

METRIC/IMPERIAL	AMERICAN
550 g/1¼ lb strong plain white flour	5 cups bread flour
1 teaspoon salt	1 teaspoon salt
50 g/2 oz butter	¼ cup butter
300 ml/½ pint milk	1¼ cups milk
2 teaspoons dried yeast	2 teaspoons active dry yeast
1 teaspoon sugar	1 teaspoon sugar
1 egg, beaten	1 egg, beaten
1 red pepper, cored, seeded and chopped	1 red pepper, cored, seeded and chopped
1 green pepper, cored, seeded and chopped	1 green pepper, cored, seeded and chopped
1 chilli, seeded and chopped	1 chili, seeded and chopped
1 onion, chopped	1 onion, chopped
1 tablespoon sesame seeds	1 tablespoon sesame seeds
rock salt	rock salt

Combine the flour and salt in a warmed bowl and leave in a warm place. Melt the butter in a small saucepan and add the milk. Warm gently but do not boil. When lukewarm, add the yeast and the sugar and leave for about 15 minutes to become frothy.

Add the yeast liquid and the egg to the flour, mix and knead together to form a soft dough. Add the chopped peppers, chilli and onion and knead into the dough. Cover and leave for 45 minutes until doubled in size.

Knock back (punch down) the dough and knead again. Divide the dough into three and shape each into a long sausage shape. Join the three pieces at one end and plait (braid) together, tucking the ends underneath

Savoury Plait (Braid)
Mixed Vegetable Fritters

at the other end. Place on a well-greased baking sheet, cover and leave to rise again for about 20 minutes.

Sprinkle the plait (braid) with sesame seeds and rock salt and bake in a preheated moderately hot oven (190°C/375°F, Gas Mark 5) for 45 minutes.
Makes 1 plait (braid)

Mixed Vegetable Fritters

METRIC/IMPERIAL	AMERICAN
1 small aubergine, thinly sliced	1 small eggplant, thinly sliced
2 courgettes, thinly sliced	2 zucchini, thinly sliced
16 onion rings	16 onion rings
8 cauliflower florets	8 cauliflower florets
1 red pepper, cored, seeded and cut into thin rings	1 red pepper, cored, seeded and cut into thin rings
oil for deep frying	oil for deep frying
Batter:	**Batter:**
100 g/4 oz plain flour	1 cup all-purpose flour
½ teaspoon salt	½ teaspoon salt
1 egg, beaten	1 egg, beaten
1 egg yolk	1 egg yolk
150 ml/¼ pint milk	⅔ cup milk

First make the batter: Sift the flour and salt together into a bowl and make a well in the centre. Add the egg and egg yolk and whisk, gradually adding the milk until the batter is smooth. Refrigerate for 1 hour.

Lay the aubergine (eggplant) slices on kitchen paper towels, sprinkle with salt and leave for 15 minutes. Pat dry, turn the slices and repeat for the other sides.

Dip the vegetables in batter, shake off excess, and deep fry in hot oil (180°C/350°F) for 5 minutes, until tender. Drain on kitchen paper and serve immediately.
Serves 8

Carrot and Banana Bread

METRIC/IMPERIAL	AMERICAN
225 g/8 oz plain flour	2 cups all-purpose flour
½ teaspoon sea salt	½ teaspoon sea salt
1 teaspoon baking powder	1 teaspoon baking powder
100 g/4 oz butter, softened	½ cup butter, softened
100 g/4 oz soft brown sugar	⅔ cup firmly packed light brown sugar
1 ripe banana, mashed	1 ripe banana, mashed
2 medium carrots, grated	2 medium carrots, grated
2 eggs, beaten	2 eggs, beaten

Sieve the flour, salt and baking powder together into a large bowl. Rub (cut) in the butter until the mixture resembles fine breadcrumbs. Add the brown sugar. Combine the mashed banana with the grated carrots and beaten eggs and add to the flour mixture. Mix well together but do not overmix as this will make the texture heavy.

Pour into a well-greased 450 g/1 lb (7 × 3 inch) loaf tin (pan) and bake in a preheated moderately hot oven (200°C/400°F, Gas Mark 6) for 1 hour or until a sharp knife inserted in the centre comes out clean. Allow to cool in the tin (pan) and serve with or without butter.
Makes 1 loaf

Corn Fritters

METRIC/IMPERIAL	AMERICAN
1 × 350 g/12 oz can sweetcorn, drained	1 × 12 oz can whole kernel corn, drained
oil for frying	oil for frying
Batter:	**Batter:**
100 g/4 oz plain flour	1 cup all-purpose flour
½ teaspoon salt	½ teaspoon salt
1 egg, beaten	1 egg, beaten
1 egg yolk	1 egg yolk
250 ml/8 fl oz milk	1 cup milk

First make the batter: Sift the flour and salt together into a bowl, make a well in the centre and add the egg and egg yolk. Whisk the eggs, gradually adding the milk and incorporating the flour. Continue to whisk until the batter is smooth and tiny air bubbles appear on the surface. Leave in the refrigerator for 1 hour.

Just before serving, stir the sweetcorn into the batter. Heat a little oil in a frying pan (skillet) and add dessertspoonfuls of the batter. Fry until golden brown on the underside, then turn and cook the other side. Drain on kitchen paper towels and serve at once.
Serves 6

Aubergine (Eggplant) in Batter

METRIC/IMPERIAL	AMERICAN
2 aubergines, thinly sliced	2 eggplants, thinly sliced
vegetable oil for frying	vegetable oil for frying
Batter:	**Batter:**
100 g/4 oz plain flour	1 cup all-purpose flour
½ teaspoon salt	½ teaspoon salt
1 egg, beaten	1 egg, beaten
1 egg yolk	1 egg yolk
250 ml/8 fl oz milk	1 cup milk
Dip:	**Dip:**
½ cucumber, peeled and chopped	½ cucumber, peeled and chopped
1 tablespoon chopped fresh mint	1 tablespoon chopped fresh mint
250 ml/8 fl oz plain yogurt	1 cup plain yogurt

Lay the aubergine (eggplant) slices on kitchen paper towels and sprinkle with salt. Leave for 15 minutes, then pat dry with more kitchen paper towels. Turn the slices and repeat for the other sides.

To make the batter, sift the flour and salt together into a bowl and make a well in the centre. Add the egg and egg yolk and whisk, gradually adding the milk and incorporating the flour. Continue whisking until the batter is smooth and small air bubbles appear on the surface. Leave in the refrigerator for 1 hour.

Heat a little oil in a large frying pan (skillet). Dip the aubergine (eggplant) slices in the batter, place in the frying pan (skillet), about six at a time, and fry gently until golden brown on the underside. Turn and cook the other side. Drain on kitchen paper towels and keep warm while cooking the remaining slices. To make the dip, stir the cucumber and mint into the yogurt. Serve with the aubergine (eggplant) slices.
Serves 8

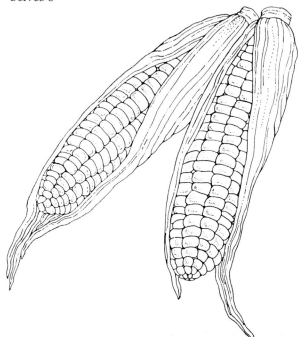

Butter Bean and Leek Rissoles

METRIC/IMPERIAL	AMERICAN
50 g/2 oz butter	¼ cup butter
1 leek, sliced and thoroughly washed	1 leek, sliced and thoroughly washed
1 garlic clove, crushed	1 garlic clove, crushed
1 chilli, seeded and chopped (optional)	1 chili, seeded and chopped (optional)
1 × 400 g/14 oz can butter beans, drained and mashed	1 × 14 oz can butter beans, drained and mashed
50 g/2 oz fresh wholewheat breadcrumbs	1 cup soft wholewheat bread crumbs
1 teaspoon salt	1 teaspoon salt
1 tablespoon chopped fresh parsley	1 tablespoon chopped fresh parsley
dash of Tabasco sauce	dash of hot pepper sauce
1 egg, beaten	1 egg, beaten
oil for frying	oil for frying

Melt the butter in a frying pan (skillet) and gently sauté the leek, garlic and chilli (if using) for about 5 minutes, until tender. Transfer to a bowl, add the butter beans and breadcrumbs and mix well. Add the salt, parsley, Tabasco (hot pepper) sauce and beaten egg. Mix and shape into small rissoles. Heat the oil in a frying pan (skillet) and fry the rissoles for about 5 minutes on each side, until golden. Serve at once with a green salad.
Serves 6

Pumpkin Bread

METRIC/IMPERIAL	AMERICAN
3 tablespoons clear honey	3 tablespoons honey
50 g/2 oz brown sugar	¼ cup brown sugar
2 tablespoons vegetable oil	2 tablespoons vegetable oil
50 g/2 oz flaked almonds	½ cup slivered almonds
50 g/2 oz raisins or sultanas	⅓ cup raisins or golden raisins
grated rind and juice of 1 orange	grated rind and juice of 1 orange
175 g/6 oz canned or mashed fresh pumpkin	1 cup canned or mashed fresh pumpkin
175 g/6 oz wholewheat flour	1½ cups wholewheat flour
2 teaspoons baking powder	2 teaspoons baking powder
1 teaspoon salt	1 teaspoon salt

Combine the honey, sugar and oil in a large bowl. Mix well and add the almonds, raisins and orange rind.

Beat in the pumpkin, then slowly sift in the flour, a little at a time, beating after each addition. Finally, add the bran that is left in the sieve, the baking powder and salt. Add the orange juice gradually, adding only enough to mix to a dropping consistency.

Turn the mixture into a well-greased 450 g/1 lb (7 × 3 inch) loaf tin (pan) and bake in a preheated moderately hot oven (200°C/400°F, Gas Mark 6) for 45 minutes or until a sharp knife inserted in the centre comes out clean. Allow to cool in the tin (pan), then turn out and serve warm or cold with or without butter.
Makes 1 loaf

Leek Burgers

METRIC/IMPERIAL	AMERICAN
50 g/2 oz butter	¼ cup butter
1 kg/2 lb leeks, sliced and thoroughly washed	2 lb leeks, sliced and thoroughly washed
1 garlic clove, crushed	1 garlic clove, crushed
100 g/4 oz fresh wholewheat breadcrumbs	2 cups soft wholewheat bread crumbs
100 g/4 oz finely chopped mixed nuts	1 cup finely chopped mixed nuts
1 teaspoon yeast extract	1 teaspoon yeast extract
250 ml/8 fl oz boiling water	1 cup boiling water
salt	salt
freshly ground black pepper	freshly ground black pepper
1 tablespoon chopped fresh parsley	1 tablespoon chopped fresh parsley
100 g/4 oz rolled oats	1 cup rolled oats
2 tablespoons vegetable oil	2 tablespoons vegetable oil

Melt the butter in a large frying pan (skillet) and sauté the leeks with the garlic until just tender and slightly reduced in size. Transfer to a large bowl and add the breadcrumbs and nuts. Dissolve the yeast extract in the water and add to the mixture. Add salt and pepper to taste and the chopped parsley, mix well and form into eight balls. Roll in the rolled oats, then pat down into burger shapes. Heat the oil in a large frying pan (skillet) and fry the burgers until golden brown on both sides. Serve immediately with a green salad.
Makes 8 burgers

Courgette (Zucchini) and Apple Bread

METRIC/IMPERIAL	AMERICAN
175 g/6 oz strong plain white flour	1½ cups bread flour
175 g/6 oz wholewheat flour	1½ cups wholewheat flour
1 tablespoon baking powder	1 tablespoon baking powder
1 teaspoon salt	1 teaspoon salt
1 teaspoon sugar	1 teaspoon sugar
1 egg, beaten	1 egg, beaten
300 ml/½ pint milk	1¼ cups milk
2 courgettes, grated	2 zucchini, grated
1 apple, cored, peeled and grated	1 apple, peeled, cored and grated
1 teaspoon caraway seeds	1 teaspoon caraway seeds

Combine both types of flour with the baking powder, salt and sugar in a large mixing bowl. Beat the egg and milk together and add to the flour mixture. Stir together briefly, then add the courgette (zucchini) and apple. Mix thoroughly but be careful not to overmix.

Turn the mixture into a well-greased 450 g/1 lb (7 × 3 inch) loaf tin (pan) and sprinkle with the caraway seeds. Bake in a preheated moderately hot oven (200°C/400°F, Gas Mark 6) for 1 hour, until well risen and nicely browned or until a sharp knife inserted in the centre comes out clean. Allow to cool in the tin (pan). Serve as an accompaniment to cheese or salad, with or without butter.
Makes 1 loaf

Onion Wholewheat Bread

METRIC/IMPERIAL	AMERICAN
750 g/1½ lb wholewheat flour	6 cups wholewheat flour
2 teaspoons salt	2 teaspoons salt
1 teaspoon sugar	1 teaspoon sugar
3 teaspoons dried yeast	3 teaspoons active dry yeast
420 ml/¾ pint lukewarm water	1¾ cups lukewarm water
3 medium onions, chopped	3 medium onions, chopped
1 tablespoon sesame seeds	1 tablespoon sesame seeds
rock or coarse sea salt	rock or coarse sea salt

Combine the flour and salt in a warmed bowl and leave in a warm place. Combine the sugar and the yeast with a few spoonfuls of the lukewarm water and leave for about 15 minutes to become frothy. Add the rest of the warm water, then pour on to the flour and knead to form a soft but not sticky dough. Add the chopped onions and knead together for a further 5 minutes. Place the dough in a warmed bowl, cover with plastic wrap and leave in a warm place for about 45 minutes until doubled in size.

Knock back (punch down) the dough and knead again. Divide into two and shape to fit two well-greased 450 g/1 lb (7 × 3 inch) loaf tins (pans). Cover and leave to rise for another 15 minutes. Sprinkle with sesame seeds and rock salt and bake in a preheated hot oven (230°C/450°F, Gas Mark 8) for 35 minutes or until golden brown and well risen. Turn out and allow to cool on a wire rack.
Makes 2 loaves

Carrot, Chestnut and Celery Rissoles

METRIC/IMPERIAL	AMERICAN
50 g/2 oz butter	¼ cup butter
2 onions, sliced	2 onions, sliced
2 garlic cloves, chopped	2 garlic cloves, chopped
2 celery sticks, finely chopped	2 stalks celery, finely chopped
2 carrots, grated	2 carrots, grated
1 × 450 g/1 lb can whole chestnuts, drained and chopped	1 × 1 lb can whole chestnuts, drained and chopped
100 g/4 oz fresh breadcrumbs	2 cups soft bread crumbs
salt	salt
freshly ground black pepper	freshly ground black pepper
1 egg, beaten	1 egg, beaten
100 g/4 oz sesame seeds	½ cup sesame seeds
oil for frying	oil for frying
1 bunch watercress to garnish	1 bunch watercress to garnish

Melt the butter in a heavy saucepan over a low heat. Add the onions and garlic and sauté gently for 1 minute. Add the celery, cover and sauté for 10 minutes, or until the celery is just tender but still a little crisp. Add the carrot, chestnuts, breadcrumbs, salt and pepper and stir together. Add the beaten egg and shape into 16 small rissoles. Dip the rissoles in sesame seeds to cover both sides.

Heat a little oil in a frying pan (skillet) and fry the rissoles, a few at a time, until brown. Keep warm in the oven until ready to serve garnished with watercress.
Serves 8

INDEX

Almonds:
  Carrot and almond loaf
    with tomato sauce 31
  Mange-tout, orange
    and almonds 56
  Split pea and almond
    soup 13
Apple:
  Courgette and apple
    bread 62
  Fennel and apple in
    cider 52
  Spinach and apple
    soup 16
Apricots:
  Coffee marinated
    mushrooms and
    apricots 21
Artichokes:
  Artichokes à la café 25
  Artichoke and celery
    soup 17
  Stuffed artichokes 26
Asparagus:
  Asparagus mousse 28
  Asparagus vol-au-vents
    24
  Cream of asparagus
    soup 12
Aspic:
  Julienne of vegetables
    in aspic 25
Aubergines:
  Aubergine and potato
    moussaka 37
  Aubergine in batter 60
  Aubergine pâté 28
  Stuffed aubergines 22
Avocados:
  Avocado dip 24
  Avocado, Mozzarella
    and tomato salad 49
  Avocado, tomato and
    smoked mackerel 19
  Guacamole 22

Bacon:
  Cabbage with bacon 54
  Dandelion salad 46
Bananas:
  Carrot and banana
    bread 60
Beans:
  Broad (Lima) beans
    and Stilton 56

Butter bean and leek
    rissoles 61
Haricot (Navy) beans
    Burgundy style 53
Mexican salad 44
Three bean casserole
    34
Three bean salad 44
Three bean soup 13
Beetroot:
  Spicy borsch 10
Bread(s) 58-62
Breadcrumbs 31, 34, 61,
  62
Broad beans and Stilton 56
Broccoli and shallots
  with black (ripe) olives
  57
Brussels sprouts:
  Purée of Brussels
    sprouts 57
Burgers:
  Leek burgers 61
Butter bean and leek
  rissoles 61

Cabbage:
  Cabbage with bacon 54
  Fruity cabbage salad
    46
  Red cabbage and pine
    nuts 51
Caesar salad 45
Candied onion soup 10
Candied sweet potatoes
  52
Carrots:
  Carrot and almond loaf
    with tomato sauce
    31
  Carrot and banana
    bread 60
  Carrot and raisin salad
    46
  Carrot, chestnut and
    celery rissoles 62
  Courgette and carrot
    pancakes 20
  Curried carrot soup 12
  Minted new potatoes,
    carrots and peas 52
  Spinach, parsnip and
    carrot layer 40
  Turnip and carrot
    purée 57

Cauliflower and fennel
    au gratin 34
Cauliflower and
    Parmesan soup 17
Cauliflower stuffing 26
Celery:
  Artichoke and celery
    soup 17
  Carrot, chestnut and
    celery rissoles 62
Cheese:
  Avocado, Mozzarella
    and tomato salad 49
  Blue cheese dip 24
  Broad beans and
    Stilton 56
  Cauliflower and fennel
    au gratin 34
  Cauliflower and
    Parmesan soup 17
  Spinach and Ricotta
    puffs 19
  Tomato and Stilton
    soup 7
Chestnuts:
  Carrot, chestnut and
    celery rissoles 62
Chinese salad 49
Chinese stir-fried
  vegetables 51
Cider:
  Fennel and apple in
    cider 52
Coffee:
  Artichokes à la café 25
  Coffee marinated
    mushrooms 21
Corn fritters 60
Courgettes:
  Courgette and apple
    bread 62
  Courgette and carrot
    pancakes 20
  Courgette and tomato
    in basil 54
  Courgettes Provençal 53
  Fettuccine with
    courgettes and
    mushrooms 38
  Leek, courgette and
    tomato quiche 37
  Stuffed courgettes 25
Cream of asparagus soup 12
Cream of mushroom
  soup 14

Crêpes 20
Crudités 24
Cucumber:
  Cucumber and potato
    soup 12
  Cucumber mousse 28
Curry:
  Curried carrot soup 12
  Vegetable curry 32

Dandelion salad 46
Dips 24
Dressings, Salad 43-9

Eggplants see
  Aubergines

Fennel:
  Cauliflower and fennel
    au gratin 34
  Fennel and apple in
    cider 52
  Leek, potato and
    fennel soup 8
Fettuccine with courgettes
  and mushrooms 38
Fritters 59, 60
Fruity cabbage salad 46

Gazpacho 9
Ginger:
  Pumpkin and ginger
    soup 9
Green pea and lettuce
  soup 14
Guacamole 22

Haricot (Navy) beans
  Burgundy style 53
Health food salad 45
Herbs:
  Herb dip 24
  Herby green salad 43
  Yogurt and herb
    stuffing 26
Hollandaise sauce 33
Hot lentil soup 14
Hot pot:
  Vegetable hot pot 41
Hummus 29

Italian-style peas 53

Julienne of vegetables in
  aspic 25

Lasagne:
  Vegetable lasagne 38
Leeks:
  Butter bean and leek
    rissoles 61
  Cauliflower and
    Parmesan soup 17
  Leek and tomato
    tartlets 29
  Leek burgers 61
  Leek, courgette and
    tomato quiche 37
  Leek, potato and
    fennel soup 8
Lemons:
  Mushroom and lemon
    salad 45
Lentils:
  Hot lentil soup 14
Lettuce:
  Green pea and lettuce
    soup 14
Liver:
  Savoury liver stuffing
    26

Main courses 30-41
Mange-tout, orange and
  almonds 56
Marrow:
  Stuffed marrow 40
Mexican salad 44
Minestrone 8
Minted new potatoes,
  carrots and peas 52
Mixed vegetable fritters
  59
Moussaka 37
Mousse:
  Asparagus mousse 28
  Cucumber mousse 28
Mushrooms:
  Coffee marinated
    mushrooms 21
  Cream of mushroom
    soup 14
  Fettucine with
    courgettes and
    mushrooms 38
  Mushroom and lemon
    salad 45
  Mushroom crêpes 20
  Mushroom timbale 36
  Olive and mushroom
    pâté 21

Okra:
  Okra Provençal 29
  Sweet and sour okra 56
Olives:
  Broccoli and shallots
    with black olives 57

Olive and mushroom
  pâté 21
Onions:
  Candied onion soup 10
  Onion wholewheat
    bread 62

Pancakes 20
Parsnips:
  Parsnip and peanut
    butter soup 16
  Spinach, parsnip and
    carrot layer 40
Pasta dishes 38
Pastry dishes 19, 24, 29,
  33, 36, 37
Pâté 21, 28
Peanut butter:
  Parsnip and peanut
    butter soup 16
Peas:
  Green pea and lettuce
    soup 14
  Hummus 29
  Italian-style peas 53
  Minted new potatoes,
    carrots and peas 52
Peppers:
  Stuffed peppers 41
Pie:
  Winter vegetable pie 36
Pine nuts:
  Red cabbage and pine
    nuts 51
Potatoes:
  Aubergine and potato
    moussaka 37
  Cauliflower and
    Parmesan soup 17
  Cucumber and potato
    soup 12
  Leek, potato and
    fennel soup 8
  Minted new potatoes,
    carrots and peas 52
  Potato salad 46
Pumpkin and ginger
  soup 9
Pumpkin bread 61
Purée of Brussels sprouts
  57

Quiche:
  Leek, courgette and
    tomato quiche 37

Raisins:
  Carrot and raisin salad
    46
Ratatouille 54
Red cabbage and pine
  nuts 51

Rice:
  Stuffed peppers 41
  Stuffed vine leaves 32
  Vegetable curry 32
Rissoles 61, 62

Salads 42-49
Sauces 33, 36, 40
Savoury liver stuffing 26
Savoury plait (bread) 59
Shallots:
  Broccoli and shallots
    with black olives 57
Side dishes 50-7
Simple starters 18-29
Smoked mackerel:
  Avocado, tomato and
    smoked mackerel 19
Soufflé:
  Spinach soufflé 41
Soups 6-17
Spicy borsch 10
Spinach and apple soup 16
Spinach and Ricotta
  puffs 19
Spinach, parsnip and
  carrot layer 40
Spinach salad 48
Spinach soufflé 41
Split pea and almond
  soup 13
Spring vegetable vol-au-
  vent 33
Sprouting salad 49
Squash:
  Stuffed marrow
    (squash) 40
Starters 18-29, 43
Stir-fried vegetables:
  Chinese stir-fried
    vegetables 51
Strudel:
  Vegetable strudel 33
Stuffed artichokes 26
Stuffed aubergines (egg-
  plants) 22
Stuffed courgettes
  (zucchini) 25
Stuffed marrow (squash)
  40
Stuffed peppers 41
Stuffed tomatoes 22
Stuffed vine leaves 32
Sweet and sour okra 56

Sweet and sour salad 48
Sweet potatoes:
  Candied sweet
    potatoes 52
Sweetcorn:
  Corn fritters 60

Tabouleh salad 48
Three bean casserole 34
Three bean salad 44
Three bean soup 13
Timbale:
  Mushroom timbale 36
Tomatoes:
  Avocado, Mozzarella
    and tomato salad 49
  Avocado, tomato and
    smoked mackerel 19
  Carrot and almond loaf
    with tomato sauce 31
  Courgette and tomato
    in basil 54
  Leek and tomato
    tartlets 29
  Leek, courgette and
    tomato quiche 37
  Stuffed tomatoes 22
  Tomato and Stilton
    soup 7
Turnip and carrot purée 57

Vegetable compote 21
Vegetable curry 32
Vegetable hot pot 41
Vegetable lasagne 38
Vegetable salads 42-9
Vegetable strudel 33
Vegetarian stuffing 26
Vine leaves:
  Stuffed vine leaves 32
Vol-au-vents:
  Asparagus vol-au-vents
    24
  Spring vegetable vol-
    au-vent 33

Waldorf salad 43
Watercress soup 17
Winter vegetable pie 36

Yogurt and herb stuffing
  26

Zucchini *see* Courgettes

ACKNOWLEDGEMENTS

The publishers would like to thank: photographer
Melvin Grey, 2-3, 6, 11, 15, 18, 30, 35, 39, 42, 58; stylist
Carolyn Russell; home economist Margot Mason.
The publishers would also like to thank the
photographers Robert Golden, 55; Roger Philips, 50.
Illustrations by Lindsay Blow